WORLD WAR II IN THE PACIFIC

WORLD WAR II
IN THE
PACIFIC

IAN BECKETT

GALLERY BOOKS
An imprint of W.H. Smith Publishers Inc.
112 Madison Avenue
New York, New York 10016

Published by Gallery Books
A Division of W H Smith Publishers Inc.
112 Madison Avenue
New York, New York 10016

Produced by
Brompton Books Corp.
15 Sherwood Place
Greenwich, CT 06830

ISBN 0-8317-6028-1

Printed in Hong Kong

10 9 8 7 6 5 4 3 2 1

PAGE 1: Pearl Harbor, 7
December 1941. The USS
Cassin lies crushed against
the USS *Downes* in a dry-
dock with the USS
Pennsylvania in the
background.

PAGES 2-3: An American
artillery crew in action
during the Solomons
campaign, 1943.

THESE PAGES: Rockets
bombarding Japanese
positions on Iwo Jima, 3
March 1945.

CONTENTS

Introduction 6

1 Onslaught in the East 12

2 Victory Disease 24

3 The Way Back 34

4 Island Hopping 50

5 Japan Defeated 64

Conclusion 77

Index and Acknowledgments 79

INTRODUCTION

Ironically, it was the United States that set Imperial Japan on the road to Pearl Harbor. When Commodore Matthew Perry's naval squadron sailed into Tokyo (then Yedo) Bay in 1853, it ended the self-imposed isolation the Tokugawa warlord *shoguns* had sought to maintain against western trading interests for over 200 years. Europeans quickly followed the US lead in forcing trading concessions, and the Japanese were compelled to recognize that only rapid development along western lines could save them from being parceled up among the great powers like neighboring Imperial China. The modernization that ensued would bring Japan to the first rank of significant powers in a remarkably short time but, in the process, it bred an ambitious nationalism, one fueled by the latent racist attitudes with which both Japanese and westerners viewed each other.

The years of the Meiji Restoration (1868-1912) saw the transformation of Japanese society with an end to feudalism, the introduction of a modern taxation system, the emergence of a centralized bureaucracy and the encouragement of industrialization. Moreover, with an army modeled on that of Imperial Germany — German-style conscription was adopted in 1873 and a General Staff six years later — and a navy modeled on that

LEFT: Commodore Perry's meeting with the emperor's commissioners at Yokohama, 8 March 1854.

BELOW: An idealized view of a naval battle off Port Arthur during the Russo-Japanese War of 1904-05.

BELOW LEFT: A naval engagement in the Yellow Sea during the Sino-Japanese War of 1894.

of Britain, Japan not only regained the freedom to manage her own commercial affairs but also began to win at least a quasi-status among the great powers whose own imperial methods the Japanese now began to emulate.

Initially, the international community resisted the process, which had begun with Japan's assumption of suzerainty over the Ryukyus from China in 1874. Later, the so-called 'Triple Intervention' by France, Germany and Imperial Russia stripped Japan of the Liaotung peninsula won from China by the Treaty of Shimonoseki which terminated the Sino-Japanese War of 1894. Japan had sought additional territories to accommodate her rapidly growing population but effectively secured only Formosa, since the Korean peninsula received its independence from China rather than passing to Japanese control. Nevertheless, Japan then participated in the relief of the diplomatic legations at Peking during the Boxer Rebellion (1900) and, in 1902, Britain compensated for her own naval weaknesses in East Asia by concluding an alliance with Japan that would enable the Royal Navy to concentrate against a possible combination of the French and Russian fleets in European waters. That alliance restrained the French from intervening in the Russo-Japanese War (1904-05) which resulted from the frictions generated by the two states' forward policies in both Korea and Manchuria, where the Russians had assumed the lease of the Liaotung peninsula. Japan did not achieve all her aims in the American-mediated Treaty of Portsmouth but she did acquire part of Sakhalin and the leases of Port Arthur and the Liaotung peninsula. The Japanese were also well placed to extend their influence over Manchuria and Korea, the latter being annexed in 1910.

Changing perceptions of the European balance of

ABOVE: Japanese artillery during the operations around Tsingtau in 1914.

ABOVE RIGHT: Japanese troops advancing into Shansi province under the shadow of the Great Wall, 30 November 1937.

LEFT: A Japanese 150mm howitzer before the German defenses of Tsingtau, 1914.

RIGHT: Shanghai in flames after a Japanese attack, 27 October 1937.

power made Japan an ally not only of Britain but also of France and Russia against Germany in 1914. Japanese forces also intervened in Russia against the Bolsheviks after the Russian Revolution and held Vladivostok until as late as 1922. The war also offered opportunities for making substantial gains at the expense of China, which had been greatly weakened by its own revolution in 1911. In 1915 the Chinese were forced to concede the '21 Demands' which extended Japanese influence over a variety of trade outlets and sources of raw materials, including the renewal, for a further 99 years, of leases in Manchuria first acquired in 1905. In addition, Japan received the League of Nations' mandate to take over former German possessions in the Pacific, notably the Carolines, Marianas and Marshalls. Japan also succeeded to German 'rights' in China itself, such as the lease of Kiaochow.

Japan had truly emerged as a state powerful enough for her ambitions to arouse considerable concern among the western powers. Accordingly, with the expiry of the Anglo-Japanese alliance in 1921, Britain and the United

States sought to bind the Japanese in a new entente which might restrain their activities. The subsequent Washington Conference from November 1921 to February 1922 required the Japanese to return Kiaochow to China and to accept a limitation on the construction of capital ships in the ratio of 5:5:3 with the United States and Britain.

Japanese acceptance of naval limitation reflected moderation within the government. However, the army and navy enjoyed control over the service ministries under the constitution adopted in 1889 – significantly, one modeled on Germany's somewhat less than democratic arrangements. The roots of democracy were shallow and the program of the political right for further expansion in search of raw materials, new markets and fresh territories gained considerable support amid an economic recession. In such circumstances, democracy fell victim to an increasing extremism which was manifest in the repeated assassination of moderates. Moreover, in September 1931 Japanese troops guarding the South Manchurian Railroad in accordance with leasehold rights initiated their own foreign policy by manufacturing the 'Mukden Incident' to seize control of that city and precipitate an occupation of Manchuria as a whole. Manchuria was proclaimed the puppet state of Manchukuo in February 1932 and Japan left the League of Nations.

The army's initiative in Manchuria was motivated primarily by the desire to act before the Chinese nationalist *Kuomintang* movement revitalized China, but the Mukden Incident also marked the end of democratic control in Japan itself. Claiming to represent the emperor, the army similarly used a clash between Japanese and Chinese troops at the Marco Polo bridge south of Peking in July 1937 to launch a full-scale war of conquest in China. In 1938 and 1939 there were to be serious clashes with Soviet troops along the frontiers of Siberia and Mongolia, the Soviet Union also being identified as a potential threat. However, having signed the Anti-Comintern Pact with Nazi Germany in November 1936 (the Comintern or Communist International being the agency through which the Soviets sought to export their brand of revolution) and a Tripartite Pact with Germany and Italy in September 1940, the Japanese concluded a Non-Aggression Pact with the Soviets in April 1941. This freed the Japanese from any immediate Soviet threat and just two months later the German invasion of Russia, of which the Japanese had no prior knowledge, further guaranteed security. Advantage had already been taken of the collapse of France in June 1940 to put pressure on the authorities in French Indochina and on

24 July 1941 Japanese troops occupied all of southern Indochina.

The United States' own economic difficulties had contributed to her course of virtual isolation since 1919. Nevertheless, there had been periodic tension between Japan and America as in 1937 when Japanese forces had fired on an American gunboat on the Yangtze. Thus, while primarily preoccupied by the war in Europe after September 1939 and edging toward a closer commitment to Britain, the Roosevelt administration did put some economic pressure on Japan from the autumn of 1940 onward, extending Lend-Lease to China in May 1941. Japan was especially susceptible to such moves since her economy was totally dependent on imported raw materials, with no less than 80 percent of her oil products being imported from the United States. There was discussion within American policy circles on the possible reinforcement of the Philippines, but the increasing commitment to the Atlantic precluded a major effort and Roosevelt did not wish to provoke the Japanese into seizing the oil-rich Dutch East Indies. Accordingly, as other restrictions were applied, oil remained exempt. But the occupation of southern Indochina led to Roosevelt freezing all Japanese assets in the United States and

placing oil exports under restrictive licenses which, by September 1941, amounted to a *de facto* embargo on goods to Japan.

Believing themselves encircled by British, Dutch and US possessions and rejecting any suggestion of withdrawing from China, the Japanese concluded that they must break the economic blockade by force. Seeking quick victories and a defendable perimeter before existing oil supplies were exhausted, they resolved to strike at both Britain and the United States simultaneously before pushing for the Dutch East Indies. Negotiations had been taking place between the US and Japan since March 1941 but it became clear from the American access to Japanese diplomatic codes, through MAGIC intercepts, that war was only a matter of time. This was especially so once a civilian prime minister in Tokyo was replaced by General Tojo in October 1941. In early November approval was given to the plan to neutralize the US Pacific Fleet at Pearl Harbor in Hawaii. Leaving an isolated anchorage in the Kuriles on 26 November 1941, the Japanese strike force was heading east when the final decision for war was taken on 1 December. Aircraft of the first attacking wave hit Pearl Harbor at 0755 hours local time on Sunday 7 December 1941.

ABOVE: The cabinet of Prince Konoye (front row, third from left) in July 1941. Then war minister, Tojo, (first left, front row) would become prime minister himself in October.

RIGHT: Emperor Hirohito inspecting his troops.

LEFT: A significant moment in the deterioration of American and Japanese relations – the USS *Panay* sinking on the Yangtze after being bombed by Japanese aircraft, 12 December 1937.

ONSLAUGHT IN THE EAST

Attacking British, Dutch and American possessions simultaneously was something of a compromise plan on the part of the Japanese. The army's attention had previously been fixed on China and the frontiers with the Soviet Union – plans for an offensive against the Soviets only lapsed in August 1941. However, the army now favored occupying the key resource areas of Malaya and the Dutch East Indies prior to engaging in hostilities with the United States. By contrast, the Japanese Navy favored striking first at the Philippines to secure the flank of any advance toward Malaya and the Indies. In August 1941, however, it was agreed that British and US forces must be attacked at the outset. Southern Thailand would be seized and a 'centrifugal offensive' launched against Malaya, Hong Kong, the Philippines, Guam, Wake and the Gilberts. Subsequently, Singapore, the Dutch East Indies and southern Burma would be targeted, before control was consolidated over the outlying parts of the Indies and the remainder of Burma.

Since the army still regarded China as the main priority, only divisions were allocated for this ambitious offensive. Three were assigned to General Yamashita's Twenty-fifth Army for Malaya and Singapore; two to General Homma's Fourteenth Army for the Philippines; two to General Iida's Fifteenth Army for Burma; and two to General Imamura's Sixteenth Army for the Dutch East Indies, of which one was first to be allocated to the reduction of Hong Kong. Some 13 divisions were retained in Manchuria and 28 in mainland China. The relatively small forces earmarked for the Pacific offensive were well supported by Japanese aircraft whose bases on Formosa, the Ryukyus and the former German islands, as well as those in Indochina, guaranteed air cover as far south as Malaya and as far east as the Philippines. However, the essential prerequisite for overall success was the elimination of the US fleet which had moved to Pearl Harbor from the American West Coast in September 1940.

The plan for the attack on Pearl Harbor conceived by the Commander-in-Chief of the Combined Fleet, Admiral Yamamoto, was slow to find favor with the navy's General Staff in view of the difficulties posed by the need to achieve total surprise. Yamamoto proposed to employ six of the navy's 10 fleet carriers to approach to within 230 miles of Hawaii, which was itself over 3400 miles from Japan, without being detected. Only the threat of Yamamoto's resignation forced final approval, and even then there were many who doubted that the plan could succeed including the strike force commander, Vice-Admiral Nagumo. The six carriers – *Akagi, Kaga, Hiryu, Soryu, Shokaku,* and *Zuikaku* – carried a total of 430 aircraft and were escorted by two battleships, two heavy cruisers, a light cruiser, 16 destroyers and three submarines on the long voyage from the Kuriles, which was accomplished without incident. Turning southeast to run down to the launching point at 2100 hours on 6 December, Nagumo hoisted the battle flag flown by the Japanese at the naval victory of Tsushima during the Russo-Japanese War. At 0600 hours on 7 December, the 183 aircraft of the first wave were launched toward Hawaii on schedule.

It had been intended to deliver a formal notification of the end of negotiations to the State Department in Washington at 1300 hours Washington time (0730 hours Hawaii time) but what was the fourteenth part of a long message was not transcribed in time by the Japanese Embassy. In fact, the Japanese ambassador, who was unaware of the import of the timing, only took the message to the State Department at 1400 hours, by which time the attack had begun. Thus, the attempt to conform with the niceties of international law by giving the Americans half an hour's warning of hostilities failed and gave additional currency to the 'Day of Infamy.' Yet, in some respects, the Japanese attack came as a welcome relief to both the British and US governments and, while a series of misunderstandings and failings in communications, command and intelligence in Washington and Hawaii contributed to the Japanese achieving total surprise, it appears an increasing possibility that Washington was not as honest as it might have been in relaying its estimation of the probability of attack to its commanders in Hawaii. Certainly, it has been suggested that, while being culpable, the Commander-in-Chief of the Pacific Fleet, Admiral Kimmel, and his army counterpart, Lieutenant General Short, both of whom had only taken up their respective appointments in February 1941, carried more than their fair share of blame for what occurred.

PAGES 12-13: Battleship Row, Pearl Harbor, showing (left to right) the USS *Maryland*, the capsized *Oklahoma* and the sunken *West Virginia* burning alongside the *Tennessee*.

LEFT: The Strike Force commander at Pearl Harbor, Vice-Admiral Nagumo of the First Air Fleet.

ABOVE RIGHT: Rescue teams at work on the USS *West Virginia*, 7 December 1941.

RIGHT: Another view of the stricken USS *West Virginia*.

LEFT: Taken at around 0800 on 7 December 1941, one of the attacking Japanese aircraft can be seen to the right of center of this view across Ford Island toward Battleship Row where a plume of smoke registers a torpedo hitting the USS *West Virginia*.

RIGHT: Despite the risk of explosions, American seamen battle to fight the flames on Battleship Row after the Japanese attack.

BELOW LEFT: The Japanese view of their principal targets at Pearl Harbor.

Some reinforcement had been effected prior to the beginning of the Japanese offensive but this did not compensate for the overall weakness of US forces in the Pacific, and American strategic plans recognized the need to remain on the defensive while the European theater took precedence. Moreover, while they were aware of the dangers of a Japanese attack on Pearl Harbor, Kimmel and Short had to balance the need to maintain a high state of readiness against the equal necessity of trying to train their largely inexperienced formations for possible war. Kimmel and Short were also confronted by the sheer volume of raw intelligence being derived from MAGIC and other sources, much of it difficult to interpret meaningfully. A war-warning was directed to Kimmel from Washington on 27 November but that, to Short, was far less specific and, in any event, both men assumed that the other had taken more precautions than was actually the case. Subsequently, on the fatal morning of 7 December, not enough importance was attached to contacts made with unknown submarines by USS *Ward* and USS *Condor*, while the detection of a large number of aircraft on the army's radar screen at Kahuka Point was put down to an expected reinforcement flight of B-17s from the United States. A final failure was the delay by Washington in conveying the alarm registered by the interception of the last part of Tokyo's message to its ambassador with the significant request that he deliver it at 1300 hours. Atmospherics made radio communication with Hawaii difficult – no one appears to have thought of trying the telephone – and it was also believed that the Philippines were more at risk than Pearl Harbor. The message finally reached Hawaii at 0733 hours local time through a commercial channel but did not get to Short's headquarters until 1500 for the simple reason that the messenger was caught in the bombing en route and had to take shelter.

The Japanese had intended to deploy torpedo-bombers against the American fleet before dive-bombers attacked the surrounding American airfields but a misunderstanding between flight commanders resulted in a simultaneous assault on both shipping and airfields. Only 79 of the 231 American aircraft on Hawaii survived being destroyed on the ground. Fortunately, the Pacific Fleet's aircraft carriers were absent, delivering aircraft to Wake – the Japanese decided to press ahead regardless – but the remainder of the fleet lay peacefully at anchor. By the time the second wave of attacking aircraft had departed the scene at 0945 hours, seven of the eight battleships in port had been severely damaged: USS *Arizona* and USS *Oklahoma* had capsized; USS *West Virginia* and USS *California* had settled upright on the bottom; USS *Nevada* had been beached; and both USS *Tennessee* and USS *Maryland* hit though not sunk. The old target battleship USS *Utah* had also gone to the bottom and the USS *Pennsylvania* was damaged in dry-dock. Three cruisers had been heavily damaged and three destroyers and a minelayer sunk. Military and civilian casualties ran to 3581 of whom 2403 were dead, including 1107 officers and men of the USS *Arizona*.

While the American carriers that were to prove so vital to the Allied war effort had escaped, the United States could not hope to match the strength of the Japanese carrier force for the time being. The situation was then made worse by the loss of the British capital ships HMS

LEFT: British seamen evacuating the sinking HMS *Prince of Wales* off the Malayan coast, 10 December 1941.

RIGHT: The nadir of British fortunes in the Far East — the capitulation of Singapore, 15 February 1942.

LEFT: The seemingly invincible advance of Yamashita's troops down the Malayan peninsula.

RIGHT: Japanese armor reaches the Cathay Buildings in Singapore City.

BELOW RIGHT: Some of the thousands of Allied troops going into Japanese captivity at Singapore.

Repulse and HMS *Prince of Wales* on 10 December. Churchill's government had decided in October to send the two ships to the Singapore naval base with four destroyers and the aircraft carrier HMS *Indomitable*, but the latter ran aground in Jamaica and after repair was then retained in the Atlantic. With the news of Japanese landings in northern Malaya, the former Vice-Chief of the Naval Staff, Admiral Phillips, resolved to strike at the invading force in the Gulf of Thailand. Most of the aging British aircraft available in Malaya had already been destroyed and Phillips therefore chose to operate without air cover. Sighted by a Japanese submarine, they were hit by four separate attacks from bombers and torpedo aircraft in a period of just over two hours, and both were sunk with the loss of Phillips and 840 officers and men before fighters from Singapore could reach them. It was the first occasion in which aircraft alone had destroyed capital ships on the open sea.

In Malaya itself the situation of the British and Imperial troops deteriorated rapidly despite the fact that

the defenders mustered 85,000 men compared to the 60,000 Japanese committed to the Malayan peninsula and southern Thailand in the early hours of 7 December 1941. The British formations were not sufficiently concentrated since it had been intended to defend Malaya primarily by air power, and many military units were allocated to dispersed airfield defense. The early loss of aircraft which simply could not match modern Japanese fighters was a critical blow. Moreover, the 11th Indian Division was also simultaneously committed to a possible advance into Thailand (Operation Matador) to forestall any Japanese offensive and was effectively caught between its two roles, faring badly in the first major engagement of the campaign at Jitra between 10 and 12 December. It recovered sufficiently to hold its positions around Kampar between 27 December and 3 January 1942 and enabled the 9th Indian Division to avoid being cut off in the east, but the British were little prepared for waging a campaign in the jungle terrain of the Malayan peninsula and, in any case, they had seriously under-

estimated the abilities of the Japanese.

On 4 January 1942 General Wavell, who had recently been appointed Commander-in-Chief in India, was appointed Supreme Commander of Allied Forces in the Southwest Pacific over the so-called ABDA (American, British, Dutch and Australian) Command based on Java in the Dutch East Indies. He ordered Lieutenant General Percival, commanding the British forces in Malaya and Singapore, to pull back to Johore where a stand might be made with the newly arrived 8th Australian Division and 18th British Division. However, continuing lack of resolution forced Percival back to Singapore island and its great naval base which the British had thought all but impregnable to attack. Another failure to concentrate the defense allowed the Japanese to get across the Straits of Johore on the night of 8 February. After losing control of the island's water supplies on the 13th, Percival surrendered two days later with over 70,000 men, some of whom had not even fired a shot, falling into Japanese hands. In all, Allied casualties in the Malayan campaign amounted to 9000 dead and wounded and 130,000 captured, while Japanese casualties were only some 9800 men. With the capitulation of the largest number of British troops in history, the myth of white supremacy in the East had been thoroughly shattered.

Elsewhere, equal success attended Japanese efforts. After 18 days of resistance, the garrison of Hong Kong, consisting of two British and two Indian battalions which had been reinforced only in November by two Canadian battalions, surrendered on Christmas Day 1941. Falling back from the initial defense position of 'Gindrinkers' Line' to the island of Hong Kong itself on the sixth day, they had been vastly outnumbered and had then run low on both water and ammunition. The defense cost the Imperial garrison some 4500 dead, with another 6500 men falling into Japanese hands. The American garrison on Guam had been overwhelmed on 10 December and, having fought off one Japanese assault on 8 December, the 449-strong US Marine de-

fenders on Wake were forced to capitulate under the weight of a second attack on 23 December, despite the comparative proximity of an American naval task force including the aircraft carrier, USS *Saratoga*. Nonetheless, they had downed 21 Japanese aircraft, sunk two warships and damaged seven more. Three days earlier, the Japanese had begun their main invasion of the Philippines following an initial aerial assault that had comprehensively destroyed the US Far East Air Force and the occupation of the outlying islands of the Philippines archipelago. Indeed, by 13 December the few surviving fighters were ordered to avoid combat and concentrate on reconnaissance while the surviving B-17 bombers were withdrawn to Australia two days later. In their main land operations, some 43,000 men of Homma's army landed in Luzon's Lingayen Gulf to be followed by a further 7000 two days later at Lamon Bay.

The Commander-in-Chief of United States Forces, Far East, (USAFFE), Lieutenant General Douglas Mac-Arthur, had only one regular division; his 10 locally raised divisions only mobilized in September 1941 were without sufficient equipment. Nevertheless, MacArthur hoped to offer a more active defense than that envisaged by prewar plans to hold just Manila Bay. It soon became clear that there was little hope of holding the Japanese everywhere and on 23 December MacArthur began conforming to the prewar plan by falling back on the Bataan peninsula and the forts in Manila Bay. Not without difficulties, the defenders had completed the withdrawal by 6 January but, despite the seeming natural strength of the ruggedly mountainous terrain, prospects were not good. Supplies were low, disease was weakening the defenders and some American policy-makers, notably in

ABOVE, FAR RIGHT: General Homma comes ashore in the Philippines, 24 December 1941.

ABOVE RIGHT: Douglas MacArthur and his chief of staff, Lieutenant-General Sutherland, outside the Malinta Tunnel on Corregidor.

ABOVE: Japanese forces in the Philippines.

LEFT: American aircraft caught on the ground at Wake Island.

RIGHT: American and Filipino troops captured on Bataan, 9 April 1942.

the US Navy, had already concluded that there was little point in trying to reinforce the Philippines from Australia. In fact, on 23 February 1942, Roosevelt ordered MacArthur to leave for Australia. With selected staff officers, he was taken by fast patrol boat to Mindanao and thence by B-17 to Australia, making his celebrated remark, 'I shall return,' when touching down at Darwin on 17 March.

In fact, the Japanese had erred in concentrating on the occupation of Manila itself rather than cutting off the American retreat into Bataan and in sending a complete division to assist in the conquest of Java a month earlier than had originally been intended. Thus, while the defenders had been forced back from their main battle position by 23 January, the Japanese then had to regroup before launching a renewed assault on 3 April. This broke the defense and on 9 April Major General King surrendered his I Corps. Some 600 Americans and between 5000 and 10,000 Filipino soldiers died on the notorious 'Death March' from Bataan to Camp O'Donnell as 78,000 men passed into captivity. Within two months a further 1600 Americans and 16,000 Filipino prisoners died at Camp O'Donnell, the barbaric Japanese treatment of captives throughout the war reflecting a code in which surrender was regarded as the ultimate disgrace and the lives of those surrendering as cheap. At least 16,000 of the 61,000 prisoners forced to work on the Burma-Siam railroad also died.

No single individual had been left in command of American forces after MacArthur's departure and the American garrison of Corregidor island therefore continued to resist. On 5 May, however, Lieutenant General Wainwright surrendered the battered island. Only 1000 Japanese were required to neutralize a garrison of 15,000 troops, but the majority were base details huddled in the Malinta tunnel complex and water had run low. To spare his men from excesses, Wainwright also surrendered the remainder of the Philippines even though other commanders were not technically subordinate to him. By 9 May all organized resistance in the Philippines had ended but a number of troops took to the mountains to wage a guerrilla campaign against the Japanese.

A similar pattern of Japanese success had meanwhile repeated itself in the Dutch East Indies. Available Allied aircraft were soon destroyed, and on 27 February Rear Admiral Doorman's *ad hoc* Combined Striking Force of five cruisers and nine destroyers was dispersed in the Battle of the Java Sea. Two cruisers, including Doorman's flagship and three destroyers, were sunk and the remainder were all eventually eliminated although the American cruiser USS *Houston* and the Australian cruiser HMAS *Perth* subsequently did some damage in the Battle of the Sunda Strait by attacking Japanese transports landing troops at Merak before they were also sent to the bottom. ABDA Command was dissolved on 25 February with Wavell ordered back to India; remaining Dutch and British forces surrendering in Java on 7 and 8 March respectively.

In Burma, Iida's Fifteenth Army had taken Moulmein by 30 January, his troops having seized the airfields at Victoria Point, Tavoy and Merjui from southern Thailand to cut off the possibility of air reinforcements being dispatched to Malaya and Singapore. Thereafter, the port of Rangoon was the key to isolating the British forces in Burma itself, since landward communication with India was all but impossible given the geographical

isolation of the country. Forced back to the Sittang River, the 17th Indian Division found itself heavily engaged and on 23 February the Sittang bridge was ordered destroyed although two brigades were still on the wrong side of the river. Wavell sacked his unfortunate former Chief of Staff in Delhi, Lieutenant General Hutton, commanding the British forces in Burma, who now counseled the abandonment of Rangoon. Hutton was replaced by General Alexander but he, too, soon decided that Rangoon could not be held. Accordingly, it was abandoned and fell to the Japanese on 9 March with Alexander only narrowly avoiding capture as the British forces retreated to the north.

With Lieutenant General Slim now commanding a re-organized Burma Corps, the British conducted an epic 1000-mile fighting retreat — the longest in the British Army's history — back across the Irrawaddy and the Chindwin Rivers. The Chinese Fifth and Sixth Armies were also driven back, and the Japanese overran the terminal of the Burma Road at Lashio on 29 April. By 20 May all Burma was in Japanese hands and they had also occupied the Andaman Islands in the Bay of Bengal. Japanese forces had also occupied the Gilberts and penetrated the Bismarcks, Solomons and New Guinea. It was a remarkable string of successes and enabled the Japanese to give effect to what had been somewhat vaguely described by the then foreign minister in August 1940 as a Greater East Asia Co-prosperity Sphere.

In the space of just six months the Greater East Asia Co-prosperity Sphere had embraced an indigenous population of over 90 million, the impact of Japanese occupation upon which cannot be emphasized too highly. The Allied defeats, especially that at Singapore, had dealt a crushing blow to the prestige of the colonial powers. And, to begin with, the Japanese appeared to offer existing nationalist groups the opportunity for in-

dependence, even if on terms dictated by Tokyo. In Burma the Japanese sponsored a Burma Independence (later National) Army in December 1941 under the command of the 26-year-old Aung San, who had left Burma for Japan in August 1940. On 1 August 1943 Burma was granted formal but, in reality, limited independence under Prime Minister Dr U Ba Maw. A similar form of independence was extended to the Philippines in October 1943 and, if the Japanese had not been defeated in August 1945, they would undoubtedly have completed their creation of KRIS, a movement aimed at the promotion of union between the Dutch East Indies and Malaya. Another Japanese creation was the Indian National Army consisting of some 20,000 out of the 45,000 Indian troops captured at Singapore. It was led by Subhas Chandra Bose, a former president of the Indian Congress Party, who had escaped from detention in Calcutta and fled to Berlin in 1941 and was then transported to Tokyo by submarine. Bose established a provisional government in Singapore and was supposedly given a nominal administrative responsibility for the Andaman and Nicobar Islands.

However, it was not long before Japanese rule began to reveal a ruthless determination to extract as much as possible in economic terms from the occupied countries. The Japanese victories had merely substituted one form of colonialism for another. At least 300,000 men and women from the Dutch East Indies, for example, were used as forced labor by the Japanese. Some nationalists used Japanese 'independence' to gain political ground or as a focus for popular opposition. In the Dutch East Indies, the Japanese initially allowed nationalist politicians such as Kusno Sukarno to establish the *Putera* ('Center of Power') organization in March 1943 but, when this developed into an anti-Japanese party, it was dissolved. Elsewhere, on the other hand, nationalist groups fought the Japanese.

In the Philippines nationalist guerrillas were incorporated into the USAFFE while prewar peasant unions and communists, many of whom had already hidden weapons in the prewar colonial period, met in March 1942 to form the *Hukbo ng Bayan Iagan sa Hapon* ('People's Anti-Japanese Army') or *Hukbalahap*. A similar pattern emerged in Malaya, where the communist-dominated Malayan People's Anti-Japanese Army (MPAJA) waged a guerrilla war against the Japanese, and in Indochina where communists led by Ho Chi Minh had been instrumental in forming the *Viet Nam Doc Lap Dong Minh Hoi* ('League for the Independence of Vietnam') or *Viet Minh* in May 1941. Such groups received support from the Allies through the agency of the US Office of Strategic Services (OSS) in Indochina or the British Force 136 in Malaya. The net result was that the experience of Japanese occupation either created or reinforced demands for future independence, making it unlikely that the old colonial powers would be able to reassert their presence easily once the Japanese were defeated.

In the short term, of course, the defeat of the Japanese was a somewhat distant prospect even given the underlying strategic weakness of Japan, but the Japanese then made the mistake of succumbing to 'victory disease.'

BELOW, FAR LEFT: An all too familiar sight in the early months of 1942 – the Rising Sun being raised over a Pacific island.

BELOW LEFT: The Stars and Stripes being lowered by the victorious Japanese on Corregidor, 6 May 1942.

BELOW: Japanese forces entering Tavoy in Burma.

VICTORY DISEASE

The initial Japanese war plan had envisaged securing a defensible perimeter at some distance from Japan itself, one to hold against the anticipated counterattacks, in the expectation of then being able to negotiate with the Allies. However, Japan's advance across the Pacific rapidly took on a momentum all its own, with various elements within the Japanese High Command putting forward their own particular schemes often in blatant contradiction to the realities of Japanese resources and capabilities.

A key player in the strategic debate was the Navy General Staff which had pressed strongly for the occupation of the Gilberts, Bismarcks and Solomons and now favored sweeping southeastward through New Guinea to the very northern coast of Australia, as well as occupying even more distant island groups as far east as the New Hebrides, Fiji and Samoa and as far north as the Aleutians. The acquisition of Rabaul on New Britain as a base was particularly significant. Originally seized to cover the approach to the Japanese base at Truk in the Carolines, Rabaul's own importance had then necessitated the advance into the Solomons, the Admiralties and New Guinea in March and April 1942. In order to consolidate control over such possessions, the Navy General Staff wanted to isolate Australia from the United States and therefore proposed to occupy Tulagi in the Solomons and Port Moresby in New Guinea.

In the meantime, Japanese carriers had not only been supporting amphibious operations throughout what was also called the Southern Resources Area but also undertaking more distant raids. On 19 February 1942 aircraft from Nagumo's 1st Air Fleet struck Darwin in Australia's Northern Territories, which had become an essential Allied base for the support of the then continuing resistance in the Dutch East Indies. Considerable damage was done to the city and the Japanese also sank a destroyer and seven other vessels, damaged a further five, and inflicted 390 military and civilian casualties, including 240 dead, for the loss of 15 of their own aircraft. On 4 March the Japanese raided Darwin again, as well as the smaller towns of Wyndham and Broome, destroying seven aircraft and 16 flying boats in just 15 minutes at the latter. Only with the arrival of three American fighter squadrons on 17 March did the Japanese raids cease.

Following further support for Japanese operations in the Indies, Nagumo's fleet, with the carriers, *Akagi*, *Hiryu*, *Soryu*, *Shokaku*, and *Zuikaku*, then raided into the Indian Ocean in conjunction with Vice-Admiral Ozawa's Malaya Force. While Ozawa's vessels attacked shipping, and aircraft from the carrier *Ryujo* bombed targets along India's eastern seaboard, Nagumo struck at Colombo in Ceylon on 5 April and at Trincomalee four days later. Nagumo's aircraft took losses but they also sank the Royal Navy carrier HMS *Hermes*, two cruisers and a destroyer. Japanese submarines also had great success, attacking and sinking 32,000 tons worth of merchant shipping on India's west coast. The Japanese might have struck even farther afield if they had chosen to do so and, in fact, there had been a major scare in Los Angeles on the night of 24/25 February when it was erroneously thought that Japanese aircraft were attacking.

Despite the navy's success, the Army General Staff was more cautious and would have preferred concentrating available troops either to finish the war in China or, alternatively, to participate in the German war against the Soviet Union. Indeed, the army had already withdrawn some formations from Southeast Asia and the Pacific but, under pressure from the Navy General Staff, the army agreed to assist in the extension of Japanese influence both to the southeast and, also, to the Aleutians. Nevertheless, it effectively vetoed any attempt on Australia or Ceylon, which was a project suggested by Yamamoto's Combined Fleet Staff. Seeking to do something rather than merely yield the initiative to the Allies, Yamamoto's staff also came up with proposals to seize Hawaii and, beyond a descent on Ceylon, an advance toward the Middle East to link up with German forces.

PAGES 24-25: The key to the Allied counter-offensive in the Pacific – American aircraft on the deck of a carrier during the Battle of the Coral Sea, May 1942.

LEFT: Lieutenant-Colonel James Doolittle with Admiral Mitscher aboard the USS *Hornet* prior to the launching of his raid on Japan, 18 April 1942.

ABOVE RIGHT: One of Doolittle's B-25s taking off from the *Hornet* en route to Tokyo.

Such schemes were somewhat illusory and the Combined Fleet Staff settled for a decisive engagement with the United States Fleet in the vicinity of Midway, whose strategic location at the western extremity of the Hawaiian Islands made it of vital importance to the Americans. There was opposition from Army and Navy General Staffs but, at this point, their minds were concentrated by the impact of the Doolittle raid.

Absent from Pearl Harbor on 7 December, American carrier groups had had little success in striking effectively at the Japanese immediately after the start of war, as the failure to attempt a relief of Wake reflected. On 17 December, however, Admiral Nimitz was appointed to replace Kimmel as Commander-in-Chief of the Pacific Fleet, with instructions to cover both the route from the United States to Australia and Hawaii. A number of forays were therefore initiated in January and February 1942 to keep the Japanese out of the eastern Pacific. Attempts were made to raid Rabaul, the Marshalls, Wake, Marcus Island and Japanese forces being landed at Lae and Salamaua in New Guinea. American submarines had also been ordered to wage an unrestricted campaign against the Japanese and, by June 1942, had accounted for 215,198 tons of merchant shipping.

But, on 18 April 1942, a far more spectacular raid was

that of Lieutenant Colonel Doolittle's 16 B-25 Mitchell bombers which were launched from the carrier, USS *Hornet* against Tokyo and three other Japanese cities on the first ever occasion in which land-based bombers were flown off an aircraft carrier at sea. It had been hoped to launch the bombers from within 450 miles of the target but the force was spotted and they had to be launched 800 miles out. None of the bombers managed subsequently to reach an airfield on the Chinese mainland under nationalist control since they were no less than 1200 miles from Tokyo – one landed in Soviet territory – and the actual physical damage was negligible, but the psychological shock in Tokyo was considerable. Three of the eight crew falling into Japanese hands were executed.

One response to the raid was to withdraw aircraft from the Solomons for the air defense of Japan and another was to step up the campaign in China to seize the nationalist airfields. Of far more consequence, however, was the approval, given on 5 May 1942, to the Combined Fleet Staff plan to seek a decisive battle with the American carriers at Midway. That operation, however, would be preceded by the deployment of the carriers *Shoho, Shokaku* and *Zuikaku* in support of the planned landings at Tulagi and Port Moresby in New

Guinea. *Shoho* formed part of the covering force for the operations under Rear Admiral Goto and the two other carriers provided a striking force under Vice-Admiral Takagi.

Radio intercepts had alerted the Americans to the threat to Port Moresby and Nimitz ordered the carriers *Lexington* and *Yorktown* into the Coral Sea to meet the Japanese under the overall command of Rear Admiral Fletcher. Taking his own carrier, *Yorktown*, Fletcher tried to intercept the Japanese landing at Tulagi on 4 May but with little result, while poor reconnaissance on both sides contributed to the US and Japanese fleets missing each other during the next two days. In the early morning of 7 May, however, Japanese carrier aircraft bombed a destroyer and an oil tanker which they had mistaken for Fletcher's carriers and, a little later, also located some of Fletcher's supporting ships commanded by Rear Admiral Crace of the Royal Navy. These were then bombed by aircraft from Rabaul.

Almost simultaneously with the attack on Crace, Fletcher's own aircraft located what they thought was the main Japanese carrier force and both *Lexington* and *Yorktown* got their aircraft away. Fletcher then intercepted a message from a Japanese reconnaissance aircraft giving the American position but, fortunately, the American aircraft came across the light carrier *Shoho* at about 1100 hours, at the very moment that its aircraft were responding to the reconnaissance report. Within minutes the *Shoho* had been sunk but Fletcher did not feel it worth attacking the carrier's escorts and, failing to find the two larger Japanese carriers, called off the search in fading light. The Japanese then attempted a strike on Fletcher's force at sunset. They not only failed to locate the American carriers but 22 out of the 27 aircraft launched were lost in dogfights with American fighters or attempting to land back on the Japanese carriers in the dark; one was even shot down trying to land on the *Yorktown* in the mistaken belief that it was Japanese.

There was no further contact until 1100 hours on 8

May, when Fletcher's aircraft finally located the *Zuikaku* and *Shokaku*, and crippled the latter sufficiently for it to need to return to Japan for urgent repairs. In turn, a Japanese attack did minor damage to *Yorktown* and more serious damage to *Lexington* before withdrawing at about 1145 hours. At 1247 hours, however, a fire broke out on board *Lexington* leading to an explosion followed by another at 1445 hours. The *Lexington* had to be abandoned at 1710 hours and a torpedo from the USS *Phelps* then finished her off at 1956 hours. The two principal attacks had involved some 121 American and 122 Japanese aircraft. Not only were the numbers thus approximately equal but the losses, too, were similar, with 66 American and 77 Japanese aircraft downed. Both sides claimed victory in the first ever carrier battle. Effectively, Coral Sea was a tactical victory for the Japanese and their fleet withdrew in the belief that they had sunk both American carriers. However, the strategic advantage lay with the United States. Yamamoto ordered the Japanese carriers back to find the Americans but it was too late. Moreover, the Port Moresby operation was now postponed. The Americans had learned to achieve a better balance of fighters, bombers and torpedo aircraft in attacking formations on an opposing fleet that was to stand them in good stead for the engagement at Midway.

The loss of the *Shoho* and the damage to the *Shokaku* made no difference to Yamamoto's typically intricate plans for the Midway operation in which he planned to divert American attention toward the Aleutians then raid Midway itself with his fast carrier fleet to draw the American carriers onto his own force and the main Japanese battle fleet. In all, Yamamoto deployed eight carriers, 11 battleships, 87 other surface vessels, 21 submarines and over 700 aircraft but they were widely separated into five different groups, with the main fleet carriers operating without benefit of the defensive firepower of the other capital ships. It was also the case that over-confidence led the Japanese to ignore the lessons of a war game they had played on 1 May, which had demon

ABOVE LEFT: The Japanese carrier *Shoho* after being torpedoed at the Coral Sea, 7 May 1942. An American aircraft can be seen dropping another torpedo to the right of the photograph.

ABOVE: Another of the Japanese carriers – probably the *Shokaku* – struck as it attempts to evade aircraft from the USS *Yorktown*, 8 May 1942.

RIGHT: The crippled USS *Lexington* soon to be abandoned and sunk.

strated the American ability to hit the Japanese aircraft carriers as hard as the Japanese could hit the Americans! Moreover, by the time the last elements of Yamamoto's fleet sailed for Midway on 29 May, US code-breakers had already correctly identified Midway as the target.

Thus, Nimitz declined to be drawn by the Aleutians diversion and hurriedly concentrated Vice-Admiral Halsey's carriers, USS *Enterprise* and USS *Hornet*, with Fletcher's USS *Yorktown*, which had to be turned round in drydock in just two days, without completing all the repairs necessary after the damage suffered at the Coral Sea. However, *Yorktown* was brought up to strength with aircrew from the USS *Saratoga*, which was undergoing repairs after being hit by a Japanese torpedo in January. An ailing Halsey was replaced by Rear Admiral Spruance, who was to prove more than equal to the approaching task. Spruance and Fletcher made rendezvous on 2 June at which time Fletcher took overall command, though the two task forces continued to operate independently.

On 3 June – the day the American code-breakers had accurately predicted as the likely date for the Japanese attack on Midway – US reconnaissance aircraft located that part of the Japanese armada allocated to the actual invasion of Midway, and land-based American bombers promptly attacked though without much effect. A second attack was also made on the same ships by flying boats in the early hours of 4 June and a Japanese tanker was hit. Despite these initial attacks, Nagumo, commanding the carriers of the Japanese 1st Air Fleet, was unaware of the proximity of the American carriers since reports had not been forwarded to him from the main Combined Fleet, which was being personally directed by Yamamoto who was flying his flag in the massive battleship *Yamato*. In any case, Nagumo's ships did not possess the more sophisticated radio equipment available to Yamamoto and did not have radar either. Accordingly, Nagumo flew off his aircraft at 0430 hours to attack Midway, approximately the same time that Fletcher launched *Yorktown*'s reconnaissance aircraft to find the Japanese carriers.

In fact, it was a flying boat from Midway that between 0545 and 0603 hours sighted both Nagumo's force and

BELOW: A Douglas SBD-III Dauntless on the deck of the *Yorktown*.

RIGHT: A view of the *Yorktown* itself from one of its own aircraft.

the aircraft heading for the island. This resulted in a furious dogfight between the Japanese and the defending American aircraft at 0616 hours, while more aircraft from Midway attacked the 1st Air Fleet without result. Consequently, Nagumo ordered another attack on Midway at 0715 hours but, before his aircraft were readied, one of his own reconnaissance aircraft spotted American ships. Nagumo resolved to attack these ships then changed his mind when two more American attacks came in, including one by B-17s. A further report at 0820 hours then indicated that the American ships included at least one carrier and Nagumo once more changed his mind and decided to attack the ships once he had recovered those aircraft now returning from the assault on Midway. He also changed course toward Midway at 0918 hours. In the meantime Spruance had launched his aircraft at 0702 hours and Fletcher started his off at 0906 hours. However, due to Nagumo's change of course, Spruance's first wave missed the Japanese carriers. The American dive-bombers turned south and the torpedo-bombers north, while the accompanying

Wildcat fighters operating at the extremity of their range simply fell out of the sky one by one as their fuel ran out.

The loss of the fighters was crucial since it left the American Douglas SBD III Dauntless dive-bombers and Douglas TBD-1 Devastator torpedo-bombers easy prey to Japanese Zero fighters, particularly when the succeeding waves from all three American carriers arrived piecemeal over Nagumo's fleet. Indeed, between 0930 hours and 1015 hours the Americans lost 37 out of 41 Devastators. However, at about 1020 hours two squadrons, comprising some 37 Dauntlesses with 1000lb bombs, arrived overhead while most of the defending Zeros were still flying at low level after disrupting the lumbering attacks by the Devastators. It was also the very moment that the decks of the Japanese carriers were full of aircraft being rearmed and refueled. Within five minutes of diving out of the skies they had fatally damaged the *Akagi, Kaga* and *Soryu. Akagi* was abandoned at 1715 hours while the already abandoned *Kaga* was consumed by an explosion at 1925 hours, just 12 minutes after the *Soryu* had also disappeared beneath the waves.

Nevertheless, Yamamoto still had four light carriers available with the main fleet and declined to give up the battle. Eighteen aircraft from the *Hiryu* found and attacked *Yorktown* at 1400 hours, of which six managed to press home the attack, scoring three hits. The carrier managed to continue to make headway but two hits from torpedoes in a second attack led to her being abandoned at 1500 hours, although *Yorktown* continued afloat until sunk by a Japanese submarine two days later. In turn, aircraft from *Enterprise* and *Hornet* hit *Hiryu* at about 1700 hours. She, too, had to be abandoned and was sunk by a torpedo from one of her escorts at 0230 hours on 5 June.

Rather than risk a night engagement with the main Japanese fleet for which their aircrews were not trained, the US carriers then withdrew. While initially contemplating trying to continue the action, Yamamoto also decided to pull back at 0255 hours on 5 June. In all, the Americans had lost 99 carrier-based and 38 land-based aircraft, a destroyer, the *Yorktown* and 307 dead but the Japanese had suffered far worse, losing four fleet carriers, 322 aircraft and 3500 men as well as the cruiser *Mikuma*, which was bombed and sunk on 5 June after being severely damaged in a collision with another cruiser. Moreover, Yamamoto had lost his decisive battle and with it Japan's superiority in naval strength. The tide in the Pacific had turned.

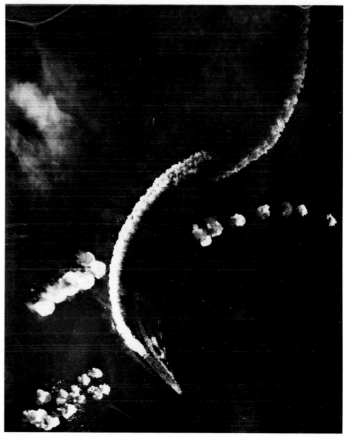

ABOVE: The Japanese heavy cruiser *Mikuma* abandoned and sinking after being attacked by aircraft from the USS *Enterprise* at Midway, 6 June 1942.

ABOVE LEFT: The *Yorktown* under attack at Midway.

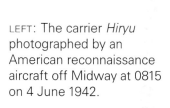

LEFT: The carrier *Hiryu* photographed by an American reconnaissance aircraft off Midway at 0815 on 4 June 1942.

RIGHT: Dauntlesses from the USS *Hornet* over the sinking *Mikuma*.

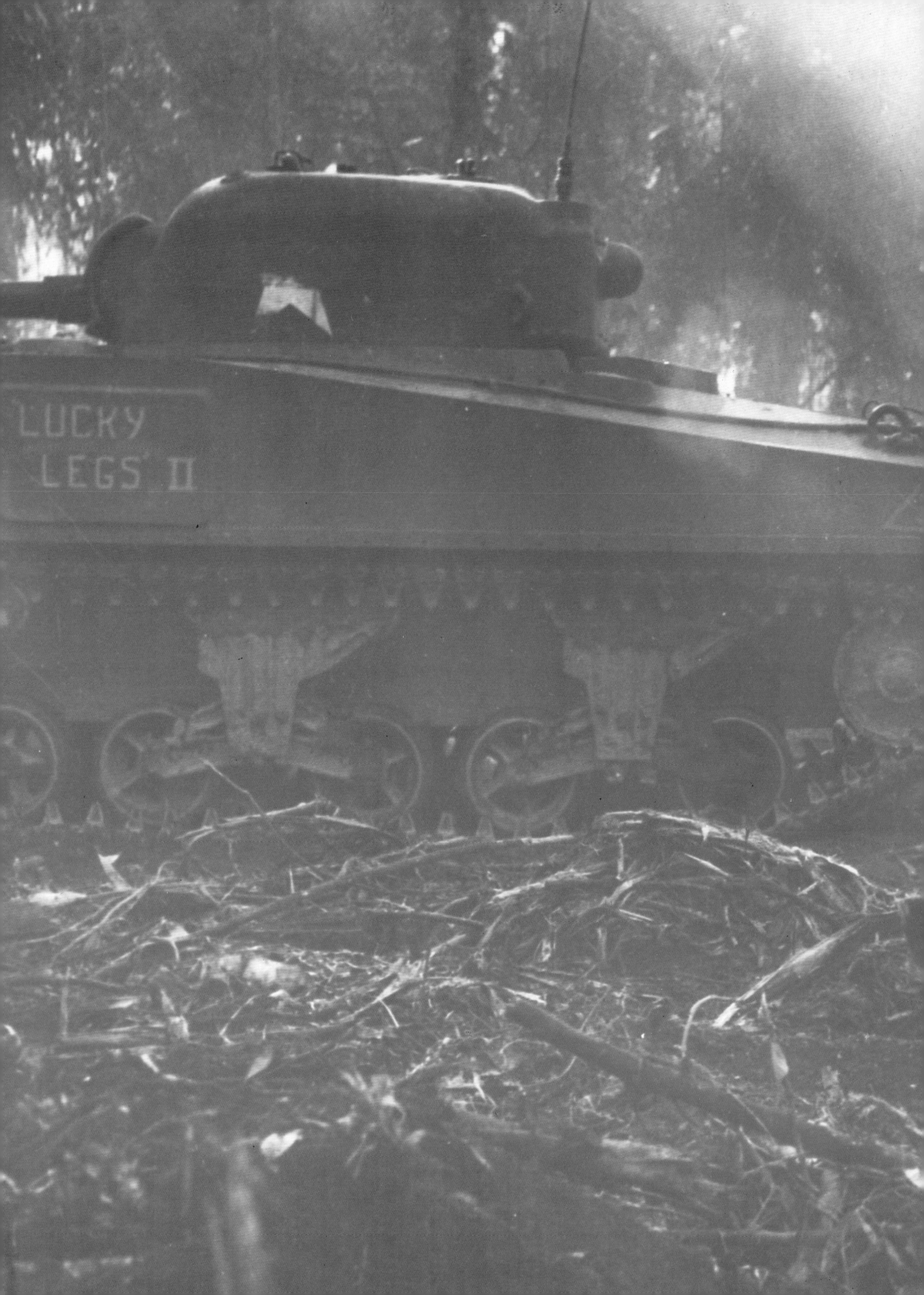
LUCKY
LEGS II

THE WAY BACK

While the United States Joint Chiefs of Staff in Washington had made the defeat of Germany rather than Japan their first priority, both the Commander-in-Chief of the US Navy, Admiral King, and MacArthur, now commanding Southwest Pacific Area from Australia, were determined to strike back at the Japanese. King, who was shortly to become Chief of Naval Operations and the navy's representative on both the Joint Chiefs of Staff Committee and the Allied Combined Chiefs of Staff Committee, suggested in February 1942 an advance toward Guadalcanal in the Solomons. MacArthur favored an active defense of New Guinea amounting to a minor offensive. Both men recognized the need to retake Rabaul on New Britain, which had provided the Japanese with such a firm base, but they differed on how to achieve this objective and, in fact, there was considerable wrangling over the respective command responsibilities of army and navy.

Accordingly, MacArthur and Nimitz, who was designated commander of the Pacific Ocean Area, were regarded equally as separate theater commanders taking overall directions from the Joint Chiefs of Staff who, in turn, directly controlled the navy's fleet carriers. The same need to balance responsibilities between the services also governed the decision, finally taken by the Joint Chiefs in July 1942, that Nimitz would move into the southern Solomons to be followed by MacArthur directing subsequent operations to seize the remainder of the Solomons and Rabaul.

PAGES 34-35: American infantrymen advancing behind a tank during the clearing operations on Bougainville in March 1944.

ABOVE: Major-General Vandergrift of the US 1st Marine Division on Guadalcanal.

LEFT: Men of Vandergrift's division photographed in August 1942.

RIGHT: Digging in around the vital Henderson Field on Guadalcanal.

It was agreed by the Joint Chiefs that Nimitz would begin to execute the first part of the strategic advance on 1 August 1942, a decision that required the urgent re-routing of Major General Vandegrift's 1st US Marine Division from New Zealand, where it would have continued training, to participate in landings at Guadal-canal and Tulagi. Indeed, the division was extremely in-experienced, practice landings off Karo in the Fiji Islands pointing up many areas for improvement. More-over, there was considerable logistic chaos when the Marines secured a beachead on Guadalcanal on 7 August and it was fortunate that there was no oppo-sition, although there was fanatical resistance by Japanese defenders at Tulagi and on the adjacent islands of Gavuatu and Tanambogo. Two days later, however, attacks by Japanese aircraft from Rabaul forced Vice-Admiral Fletcher, who was commanding the operation, to withdraw the carriers – *Enterprise, Sara-toga, Hornet* and *Wasp* – due to the difficulty of maneu-vering them safely in confined waters. Other supporting warships were also pulled out after Vice-Admiral Mikawa slipped seven cruisers and a destroyer through Rear Admiral Crutchley's destroyer screen off Savo on the night of 8/9 August. The Japanese sank a destroyer and the cruisers RNAS *Canberra,* USS *Vincennes,* USS *Quincy* and USS *Astoria* in little more than half an hour although they did not get to the transports they had in-tended to attack.

The sudden departure of the American fleet, including transports with the bulk of the logistic support required to sustain Vandegrift's division ashore, left the Marines bereft of close air support as well as supplies. However, they had secured Henderson Field by 18 August and, two days later, 19 Wildcats and 12 Dauntlesses were flown in from carriers to provide some relief from Japanese air attack and bombardment by Japanese warships. Fortui-tously, in view of the Japanese decision to order their Seventeenth Army to retake Guadalcanal, the Marines had also steadily strengthened their perimeter defenses by the time the leading Japanese elements came ashore that same day. Thus, the initial Japanese attack across the Tenaru and Ilu Rivers on 21 and 22 August was beaten off and the Japanese commander, Colonel Ichiki, committed suicide in disgrace.

But further Japanese reinforcements were conti-nually passed down the island chain by night. Fore-warned of this 'Tokyo Express' down the 'Slot' route by clandestine Allied coastwatchers, who gallantly reported by radio on Japanese movements from their hiding places, Fletcher moved to intercept the Japanese on 23 August. American aircraft missed the Japanese fleet but on the following day located and sank the light carrier *Ryujo* and damaged a seaplane carrier. However, *Ryujo* was actually deployed ahead of the main Japanese force as bait to draw in the Americans. An American recon-naissance aircraft spotted the carriers *Zuikaku* and *Shokaku,* but was unable to divert the attack on the *Ryujo* in time. Japanese carrier aircraft damaged *Enter-*

LEFT: A photograph of a naval landing party taken from a captured Japanese on Guadalcanal.

RIGHT: The USS *Wasp* after being torpedoed on 15 September 1942.

BELOW: Japanese dead after the action at 'Bloody Ridge' on Guadalcanal, 13-14 September 1942.

BELOW RIGHT: The USS *Hornet* hit at the Santa Cruz engagement, 27 October 1942.

prise. Saratoga was damaged by a torpedo fired from a Japanese submarine seven days later.

Coinciding with almost daily air attacks on the Marine positions at Guadalcanal, another major Japanese attack was launched on 12 September which progressed to within 1000 yards of Henderson Field but was beaten back from 'Bloody Ridge' by the US 1st Marine Raiders and Marine paratroopers who had been brought over from Tulagi initially to raid Taivu from which Ichiki's offensive had been launched. The Americans were successful in pushing in more reinforcements to Vandegrift but at the cost of the carrier *Wasp* on 15 September. Yet another major Japanese offensive was hurled against the Americans on 22 October but was again repulsed in an intense three-day battle.

Meanwhile, naval clashes continued. The Americans sank a Japanese cruiser and a destroyer off Cape Esperance on 11/12 October in a clash between the rival escorts of two convoys. There was another clash off Santa Cruz on 26/27 October when the Japanese moved forward to fly in carrier aircraft to Henderson Field if it was taken in the latest land offensive. In what had become almost a pattern of carrier warfare, both fleets had aircraft in the air simultaneously. The Americans severely damaged the fleet carrier *Shokaku* and the light carrier *Zuiho* but, in turn, Japanese aircraft damaged *Enterprise* and left the *Hornet* a blazing hulk to be sunk later by a Japanese warship. The damage to the American fleet temporarily left it without a single operational carrier.

Both Japanese and Americans were now fully aware of the vital significance of the struggle around Guadalcanal and, indeed, two American divisions were diverted from the European theater in October to ensure success, while the Japanese diverted formations from Korea and China. As both sides began to push these into Guadalcanal there was another fierce naval action, known as the naval Battle of Guadalcanal, between 12 and 15 November culminating in the battleships USS *Washington* and USS *South Dakota* sinking the Japanese battleships *Kirishima* and *Hiei*. The battle left the US Navy in command of the seas around the Solomons, although the Japanese managed to sink one American cruiser and damage three others for the loss of one destroyer sunk and one damaged in an action off Tassafaronga on 30 November. On land, the 1st Marine Division was relieved in early December 1942. An offensive on 10 January 1943 by the 2nd Marine, 25th Infantry and Americal Divisions, comprising Major General Patch's XIV Corps, coincided with the withdrawal of the Japanese from Guadalcanal to the northern Solomons and New Guinea. The Americans had suffered approximately 5800 battle casualties in the land campaign while the Japanese had had some 14,000 casualties from battle and at least 9000 dead from disease. Some 1000 Japanese were taken pri-

ABOVE LEFT: The transport USS *President Jackson* turning under Japanese attack during the naval battle of Guadalcanal on 12 November 1942.

LEFT: US Naval transports anchored off Guadalcanal, 4 November 1942.

ABOVE: The bodies of Japanese defenders on a Guadalcanal beach, December 1942.

RIGHT: Lieutenant-General Hyakukate of the Japanese Seventeenth Army outside his headquarters at Rabaul, October 1942.

soner while approximately 13,000 were evacuated by 9 February 1943 when the campaign finally ended.

The Japanese decision to cut their losses and withdraw from Guadalcanal had been partly influenced by a desire to reinforce the effort to take Port Moresby in New Guinea. The operation had been postponed, of course, as a result of the Coral Sea battle and a naval approach was then ruled out by the defeat at Midway. On 11 July, however, Lieutenant General Hyakutake of Seventeenth Army was ordered to advance to Port Moresby from Buna on the northern coast of New Guinea across the Owen Stanley mountains by way of the Kokoda Trail. By this time, however, MacArthur had moved to secure Port

Moresby as a base for his own endeavors, once Nimitz had taken Guadalcanal, and in May and June 1942 Australian units had arrived under the command of General Sir Thomas Blamey. MacArthur also desired to establish a forward air base across the mountains in order to counter the Japanese airfields at Lae and Salamaua and chose Buna as the location. Following various reconnaissances toward Buna, Lae and Salamaua, MacArthur ordered an advance to Buna on 15 July with the expectation of reaching the northern coast by early August. But, in pursuance of their own aims, the Japanese landed at Buna on 21 July and began moving south down the Kokoda Trail at the same time that the Australians were moving north. A savage struggle was to ensue after the first clash on the trail on 16 August.

MacArthur pushed more troops into Port Moresby and Milne Bay but on 25 August the Japanese landed at the latter and were not dislodged until 5 September. However, the Japanese drive down the Kokoda Trail was halted by the need to send troops to Guadalcanal and Australian troops were able to take Kokoda itself on 2 November 1942. MacArthur now proposed to supplement the drive across the trail with another across the mountains to Jaure and a push from Milne Bay, but it

was only with difficulty that these subsidiary operations were accomplished over even more difficult terrain than that faced by the Australians on the trail. The advance toward Buna also coincided with renewed Japanese determination to hold the northern coast. Between 19 November and 1 December the 7th Australian Division, the 32nd US Infantry Division and the so-called Warren Force were all thrown back from skillfully constructed Japanese defenses.

The commander of 32nd Division was relieved and operational control over the Americans given to Lieutenant General Eichelberger of the US I Corps. However, the Australians broke into Gona on 9 December and a reinforced Warren Force broke through at Cape Endaiadere on 18 December to link up with the Americans. In turn, the Americans pushed close to the coast and the Japanese withdrew rather than be caught between the three Allied forces, Buna falling on 2 January 1943. Some 2100 Japanese troops escaped along the coast to Lae and Salamaua but the campaign had cost them an estimated 13,000 casualties. At the cost of over 8500 battle casualties of their own – in addition to considerable losses from disease – the Allies had now cleared the way for further operations in New Guinea.

RIGHT: Australian troops firing a mortar behind which an Australian-manned American light tank is advancing during the battle for Buna in New Guinea, December 1942.

BELOW RIGHT: An Australian officer poses beside a knocked out Japanese tank at Milne Bay, New Guinea.

LEFT: Warily approaching a Japanese dugout in New Guinea, 3 January 1943.

Success at Guadalcanal had also cleared the way for further operations in the Solomons but, in fact, the Allied strategic planners were as yet doubtful as to whether they could realistically hope to take Rabaul during 1943. Consequently, it was decided on 28 March that MacArthur should cooperate with Vice-Admiral Halsey, who had succeeded to command of the South Pacific Area in October and directed the closing stages of the Guadalcanal campaign, in limiting objectives to clearing the Solomons, western New Britain, and Lae and Salamaua on the New Guinea coast. This would enable airfields to be established in range of Rabaul with the intention of tackling that target itself in 1944. Accordingly, Blamey's Australians were given the responsibility of taking Lae and Salamaua, Lieutenant General Krueger's American forces that of taking western New Britain, and Halsey that of taking New Georgia and Bougainville.

The US 41st Infantry Division had already begun to move along the New Guinea coast and in January 1943 the Australian 3rd Division had also pushed to Wau. The Japanese tried to push reinforcements into New Guinea but in March 1943 in the Battle of the Bismarck Sea they lost 10 transports and four escorting destroyers to American air attack. The overall Allied advance toward Lae and Salamaua began at the end of June with the unopposed seizure of Kiriwina and the Woodlarks. Salamaua fell to a combined Australian and American force on 12 September and, after an amphibious landing to the east, Lae on the 16th. This was followed by the occupation of Finschhafen on 2 October after another amphibious landing, and American forces from Krueger's 32nd Infantry Division were then landed at Saidor on 2 January 1944 some 100 miles ahead of the Australian advance along the coast.

The US 1st Marine Division, which had been recuperating from the Guadalcanal operations in Australia, effected a landing at Cape Gloucester on New Britain on 1 December and secured the western part of the island to a line stretching south from the airfield at Talasea. It was decided to bypass the Japanese garrison at Kavieng on New Ireland and the US 1st Cavalry Division went on instead to land on the Admiralties on 29 February, although the islands were not fully secured until May 1944. Much of the consolidation was left to Australian troops as in the case of New Britain, where the Australian 5th Division was made responsible for containing the Rabaul garrison since it had been concluded as early as July 1943 that isolation would serve as well as actual occupation in neutralizing the base.

Meanwhile, the American campaign had also proceeded in the Solomons; again with the invaluable assistance of the mainly Australian coastwatchers. Russell Island had been taken in February 1943 (Operation Cleanslate) and then Halsey had landed the US 43rd Infantry Division on the main island of New Georgia (Operation Toenails) on 5 July 1943, following preliminary landings on other islands in the New Georgia group. New Georgia was reinforced by the Japanese but Halsey, in turn, committed more troops including the US 37th Infantry Division, and after fierce fighting his forces took Munda Point on 5 August. Bypassing the Japanese garrison on Kolombangara Island, Halsey then landed on

ABOVE: The first Americans ashore from the 43rd Infantry Divison at Rendova on New Georgia take cover, 5 July 1943.

RIGHT: Marines searching for snipers on Russell Island, 23 February 1943.

Vella Lavella on 15 August. With the Japanese evacuating New Georgia and other isolated garrisons, operations were subsequently mounted against Treasury Island by the New Zealand 8th Brigade Group (Operation Goodtime) and against Choiseul Island by the US 2nd Marine Parachute Battalion on 28 October (Operation Blissful).

Such operations, especially that against Choiseul from which the Marines withdrew on 3 November, were partially designed as diversions for the landing on Bougainville, the largest island of the Solomons. The element of surprise when the US 3rd Marine Division was put ashore on Bougainville on 1 November (Operation Cherry Blossom) was also heightened by the choice of Empress Augusta Bay, which was undefended by the Japanese due to the difficult local surf conditions. The Japanese tried to disrupt the landings with both air and

ABOVE LEFT: Seabees laying steel mats during the construction of an airfield on Bougainville, December 1943.

ABOVE; Debris including a Japanese aircraft on a Bougainville beach.

LEFT: Construction materials being brought ashore on a Pacific island.

RIGHT: Marine artillerymen with a 75mm pak howitzer at Torokina on Bougainville, 15 December 1943.

BELOW: Marine PBJ bombers raiding Rabaul in early 1944.

LEFT: Marines huddled by the shoreline on Bougainville, 30 November 1943.

RIGHT: Marines viewing a tank caught in a Japanese ambush at the junction of the Piva and Numa-Numa trails on Bougainville, 14 November 1943.

naval attack but by 26 December the vital Japanese airfields had been captured at comparatively little cost despite the difficulty of getting at the deep Japanese bunkers. Thereafter, the campaign itself continued until March 1944. By that time Halsey had also occupied Green Island and Emirau Island.

The net result of the Allied campaign in the Southwest Pacific in 1943 was to effectively isolate and neutralize Rabaul which, like the Japanese base at Truk, was being increasingly subjected to sustained attack from the airfields taken or otherwise established on the captured islands. Indeed, over 250 Japanese aircraft were caught on the ground at Truk by American carrier aircraft on 16/17 February 1944, with 15 warships and over 137,000 tons of merchant shipping also sent to the bottom. As a result, the Japanese fleet was withdrawn from Truk and all naval aircraft from Rabaul. The withdrawal decision was taken by a new Commander-in-Chief of the Combined Fleet, Admiral Koga, for Yamamoto had himself

fallen victim to American airpower. Following American interception of his itinerary, Yamamoto's aircraft had been ambushed and shot down on 18 April 1943 while en route from Truk to Bougainville.

By the time of Yamamoto's death it was already clear that the great gamble of December 1941 had run its course. Despite the construction of 11 new carriers in 1941 and 1942, Japanese losses meant that they still had only 11 in commission in 1943, of which only one was a fleet carrier. Japan had also lost the cream of her pilots. American aircraft output was not only more than four times greater but firms were also producing better aircraft such as the P-38 Lightnings that had ambushed Yamamoto. Loss of merchant shipping to Allied submarines had increasingly disrupted the import of raw materials from captured territories and Japan's oil reserves were running low. Now, too, the Allies were poised to sweep across the Central Pacific toward the Philippines, China and Japan itself.

ISLAND HOPPING

The further operations in the Solomons and New Guinea for the isolation of Rabaul formed only one part of the Allied strategy for the Pacific theater in 1943. At the Casablanca Conference of Allied leaders in January 1943 Admiral King had proposed driving across the Central Pacific from Rabaul to the Philippines by way of Truk and the Marianas, which were of particular strategic value in that they commanded the routes from Japan to the Philippines and the other outposts of the Greater East Asia Co-prosperity Sphere in the southwestern ocean.

MacArthur for one opposed King's Central Pacific strategy on the grounds that he considered the New Guinea route the most appropriate approach to the Philippines, the regaining of which was always uppermost in his mind. But the British also expressed some concern at Casablanca that the ambitious nature of King's program would divert resources from the defeat of Germany and they were to argue for modifications at the subsequent Trident Conference at Washington in May 1943 and the Quadrant Conference at Quebec in August 1943. Nevertheless, there was obvious merit in a Central Pacific offensive since this was the shortest route to the Philippines and it would maximize American amphibious resources in attacks upon island groups that would be smaller and less well defended than those in the Southwest Pacific. It also offered the opportunity of establishing air bases within range of the Japanese homeland which might actually negate the need to invade the Philippines at all. At the same time, the Allies might also be in a position to move into the South China Sea toward Formosa or even Hong Kong.

Accordingly, a slightly modified version of King's original plan was adopted at the Trident Conference, one envisaging operations by the British in Burma and by the Americans against the Aleutians with a continuing drive in the Solomons and New Guinea, and a Central Pacific thrust toward the Marshalls and the Carolines. In reality, amphibious resources were not sufficient to sustain both the operations against the Marshalls as well as MacArthur's and Halsey's continued offensives in the southwest. One consequence was that decision in July 1943 to isolate rather than occupy Rabaul. Another made at the same time was that the smaller Gilberts should be attacked before the Marshalls. Ratified at the Quadrant Conference, the strategy in the Central Pacific thus emerged as an assault on the Gilberts scheduled for 15 November 1943 to be followed by operations against the Marshalls in January 1944 and against the Carolines in June 1944.

Other than the continued advances in the southwest, the first fruit of the agreed Pacific strategy was the reoccupation of those parts of the Aleutians which the Japanese had seized in 1942, primarily the islands of Attu and Kiska on which airfields had been constructed. On 11 May 1943 the US 7th Infantry Division of Admiral Rockwell's North Pacific Amphibious Forces — it represented the only other division specially trained in amphibious warfare apart from the three Marine divisions currently in the Southwest and South Pacific — landed on Attu and secured it by the end of the month. The next stage was the invasion of Kiska on 15 August but, in fact, the Japanese had evacuated its garrison on 28 July. Thus, the Americans had secured the flank for

their operations farther to the south and had also re-opened another supply route between the United States and the Soviet Union.

At this time, Japan still greatly feared Soviet inter-vention and, of course, China and Manchuria continued to swallow considerable Japanese resources. Unfortu-nately, for the Americans, however, while the Japanese could spare few additional resources for the defense of the coral atolls of the Central Pacific, they had worked hard to fortify them with bunkers and other strong-points, and they were determined to hold them to the last. Indeed, the first American target of the Gilberts was a case in point. The island group lay outside the line identified by the Japanese in September 1943 as being absolutely essential to the defense of the homeland itself – that ran from the Kuriles to Burma through the Bonins, the Marianas, the Carolines, western New Guinea and the so-called Malay barrier comprising Malaya itself, Sumatra, Java and the island chain run-ning east to Timor. But the Gilberts had been reinforced following an attack by the US 2nd Marine Raider Batta-lion during the Guadalcanal campaign in August 1942 to a strength of 4836 men including approximately 3000 combat troops drawn from the III Special Base Force and the VII Special Naval Landing Force. Moreover, the largest atoll of the group – Tarawa – was also formidably fortified on the Betio spit, with concrete bunkers covered by coconut logs and sand which made them all but im-penetrable even to a direct hit. Tarawa, which had an airfield, and the smaller and less well defended atoll of Makin with its seaplane anchorage, had been chosen as the invasion target in September 1943 in preference to

another atoll – Nauru – which appeared to offer espe-cially difficult terrain. The task of reducing them was that of Vice-Admiral Spruance's Central Pacific Force, which mustered no less than 11 carriers – five of them light carriers – and over 27,000 combat troops of Major General Julian Smith's 2nd Marine Division and Major General Ralph Smith's 27th Infantry Division operating under the overall command of yet another major general with the same surname, Holland 'Howling Mad' Smith.

Raids on Rabaul, the Marshalls and other targets be-tween September and November 1943 hit at Japanese ships and aircraft to effectively prevent any interference with the operation. Units from the 27th Infantry Divi-sion met relatively little opposition on Makin where they landed at 0831 hours on 20 November. The atoll was secured by 1130 hours on the 23rd with the only major casualty of the operation being the escort carrier USS *Liscomb Bay,* which was torpedoed by a Japanese sub-marine on 24 November. But on 'Bloody Tarawa,' it was a very different story as the 2nd Marine Division went ashore at 0910 hours on 20 November.

The Marines discovered that the preliminary naval bombardment had not subdued the defenders even if it had knocked out most of the Japanese artillery pieces. Unfortunately, the tide proved too low for the LCVPs (Landing Craft, Vehicle, Personnel) and LCMs (Landing Craft, Mechanized) to reach the shoreline, while many of the amphibious armored tractors or LVTs (Landing Vehicle, Tracked) could not surmount the Betio seawall. Forced to wade ashore without either physical protec-tion or sufficient close fire support from aircraft or ships offshore, many Marines were cut down at the water's

PAGES 50-51: Aircraft on the USS *Cowpens* during the operations against the Gilberts.

LEFT: Part of the American fleet at anchor at Atak during the campaign for the reconquest of the Aleutians.

RIGHT: Men of the US 7th Infantry Divison on Attu in the Aleutians, May 1943.

edge. Tackling the bunkers in such circumstances proved slow and costly before tanks could be brought ashore later and the operation was hampered throughout by constant failure of communications at all levels. There was also the resistance of the Japanese with which to contend despite the fact that they also suffered from the loss of their communications network due to the American bombardment and could not mount a coordinated counterattack. As a result of the difficulties, the Betio position was not secured until 1312 hours on 23 November. By the time the rest of the atoll had been secured two days later, only 146 of the Japanese garrison were still alive and most of these were Korean laborers who had made up the balance of the defenders. The Marines had suffered 3301 casualties including 984 dead in their first major amphibious assault but many vital lessons had been learned.

At the two Allied meetings at Cairo and Tehran in December 1943, collectively known as the Sextant Conferences, the Central Pacific offensive was accorded equal priority with operations in the Southwest Pacific, and the Pacific generally was recognized as the second most important theater after Northwest Europe, a decision effectively relegating the Mediterranean and Southeast Asian theaters to much less significance. The practical result was to divert more resources to the Central Pacific as the Americans prepared to take the Marshalls. Choosing to bypass some of the stronger Japanese garrisons in the group such as Jaluit and Wotje, Nimitz elected to attack Kwajalein. His subordinates were not convinced of the wisdom of going straight for Kwajalein and Nimitz was persuaded by Spruance to include Majuro, which had potential as a fleet base.

On this occasion, LCI(G)s (Landing Craft Infantry,

ABOVE: Men from the US 2nd Marine Division marching back to embark at the pier on Tarawa after their relief, 23 November 1943.

ABOVE RIGHT: An F6F Hellcat makes a hard landing on the USS *Cowpens* during the operations for the Gilberts, November 1943.

LEFT: A flight deck scene on the USS *Monterey*, late 1943.

RIGHT: Pilots being briefed for a mission over the Gilberts, November 1943.

Gunships) with rapid-firing cannon and rockets, LVT(A)s (Landing Vehicles, Tracked, Armored) – sometimes known as amphibious tanks – and the celebrated DUKW amphibious transports were available to give adequate fire support and protection to the attacking forces. The Marines were also to be better equipped with communications and better trained in cooperation with other arms, while they would also have the use of flamethrowers. Equally, the navy had also perfected its techniques for integrating the actions of a variety of naval task groups for bombardment, transport, floating supply, air support, salvage and actual assault. Moreover, the airfields on the Gilberts were rapidly brought into operation and strikes launched against the Marshalls which, in combination with carrier actions, eliminated Japanese air power in the area.

On 31 January 1944 Majuro was found to be undefended, while other small islands were also secured easily and used to land artillery to support the main operation against Roi, Namur and Kwajalein. The main assault on these went in on the following day with the 2nd Marine Division taking Roi and Namur and the 7th Infantry Division landing on Kwajalein. The latter met more determined resistance as it proceeded inland on subsequent days but all was secure by 7 February. Nimitz resolved to leap ahead to take Eniwetok atoll to the west, landing the 22nd Marines and 106th Infantry there on 18 February while, as previously related, the main carrier force struck at Truk and devastated the Japanese shipping and aircraft based there. While the

ABOVE: Secretary of the Navy, James Forrestal (second left), with the victorious commanders of the campaign in the Marshalls, 2 February 1944, including Admiral Spruance (first left) and Major-General Schmidt (fourth left).

RIGHT: American troops advancing on Kwajalein, 31 January 1944.

ABOVE LEFT: The beach at 'Bloody' Tarawa, 20 November 1943.

LEFT: The crew of an LST prepare to launch LVTs for the assault on Roi Island in the Marshalls, 2 February 1944.

Japanese had shown the now expected resistance in the Marshalls, their largest garrison – that on Kwajalein – had comprised only some 5000 men and they had been literally overwhelmed by the force brought against them. The garrisons on those islands not attacked were now to be contained by American air power until the end of the war, while the new fleet bases established at Majuro and Eniwetok could be used for yet further operations.

Originally, it had been intended that further operations should be aimed at the Carolines but the Sextant Conferences had established a preference for seizing the Marianas from which B-29s could reach Japan. However, there were those who had argued that Truk should be taken. MacArthur remained firmly committed to a triumphant return to the Philippines and urged that more resources be put into his operations in the Southwest Pacific. The damage done to the Japanese at Truk lessened the need to actually attack it in much the same way that the isolation of Rabaul negated the need to attack there either. Therefore, in March 1944 the Joint Chiefs of Staff decided that, while MacArthur should continue his operations with a tentative date of November 1944 set for a landing on Mindanao in the southern Philippines and a landing either on the main island of Luzon or, alternatively on Formosa, in February 1945, the operation against the Marianas should go ahead in June 1944 to be followed by the Palaus and the Carolines in September.

RIGHT: An F6F Hellcat being catapulted from the USS *Monterey* off the Marianas, June 1944.

BELOW RIGHT: The Japanese carrier *Zuikaku* trying unsuccessfully to evade American bombs at the Battle of the Philippine Sea off Saipan, 19 June 1944.

ABOVE LEFT: Hitting the dirt on Eniwetok, 18 February 1944.

LEFT: Wreckage and supplies lie on Kwajalein after its capture, February 1944.

It was Nimitz' hope that the Marianas operation would entice the Japanese fleet into an engagement. In fact, the Japanese had failed to perceive the Marianas as the next likely American target – they anticipated that the Palaus or Carolines would be attacked and they were also misled by the Americans' extensive preliminary carrier operations embracing Truk, the Palaus, Wake and the Marianas as well as MacArthur's operations in the southwest. Indeed, much-needed Japanese air power was diverted to western New Guinea. Nonetheless, the Japanese had formulated a plan of their own to use carriers to lure away the American carriers so that they could attack any invasion force off the Palaus with their own main battle fleet. The Americans were aware of the risk and, when the 2nd and 4th Marine Divisions began landing on Saipan in the Marianas on 15 June 1944, Spruance kept his 12 aircraft carriers as close to the beachhead as possible. Four days later, when the Japanese threw 430 aircraft at the fleet, only 102 survived massed defensive firepower and American fighters; a further 50 land-based Japanese aircraft were also lost. Moreover, the Americans also located and sank the carriers *Shokaku* and *Taiho* on 19 June and the carrier *Hiyo* on the following day. Four other carriers including the *Zuikaku* and *Chiyoda* were damaged. What was known officially as the Battle of the Philippine Sea and more popularly among American pilots as the 'Great Marianas Turkey Shoot' was the last and largest carrier battle of the war, marking the effective end of the Japanese naval air arm.

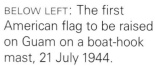

LEFT: Men from 4th Marine Division hurling grenades at a Japanese strongpoint on Saipan.

RIGHT: Marines crawling across the beach at Saipan under Japanese fire, 15 June 1944.

BELOW LEFT: The first American flag to be raised on Guam on a boat-hook mast, 21 July 1944.

BELOW RIGHT: Marines view some of the 117 Japanese killed during an early morning attempt to recapture Aslito airfield on Saipan.

On land, the newly promoted Lieutenant General Holland Smith's V Amphibious Corps was tasked with taking Saipan and Tinian while Major General Geiger's III Amphibious Corps would tackle Guam. As already indicated, the Japanese were not expecting any attack but their three garrisons totaled over 55,000 men to face the 105,000 Americans of the assaulting divisions, and they occupied well-prepared positions. In the case of Saipan, the initial assault on 15 June was far from easy and it took until 9 July to secure the island, Smith being forced to commit his corps reserve of the 27th Infantry Division. Unfortunately, the introduction of the army division exacerbated a dispute between the Marine Holland Smith, and the 27th's army commander, Ralph Smith, which had been simmering ever since the Marine had accused the soldiers of being too slow on Makin in the Gilberts and Eniwetok in the Marshalls. It now culminated in Ralph Smith's dismissal.

The Marines were then shifted to Tinian on 24 July, the 2nd Marine Division making a diversionary feint off Tinian town while the 4th went ashore in the north. Tinian was secured by 1 August although Japanese continued to emerge from hiding places to launch desperate attacks. Indeed, the closing stages of the fighting on both Saipan and Tinian was characterized by mass suicides among both Japanese soldiers and civilians, both the Japanese ground commander on Saipan, General Yoshitsugu, and the commander of the Central

Pacific Area Fleet, Vice-Admiral Nagumo, who had his headquarters on Saipan, being among a large group that leapt to their deaths from the cliffs.

Due to the unexpected delays in getting ashore on Saipan, the assault on the most important objective in the Marianas – Guam – was delayed until 21 July when Geiger's 3rd Marine Division landed at Asan and the 1st Marine Brigade, reinforced by 77th Infantry Division, at Agat. The now customary *banzai* counterattacks were encountered but Guam was declared secure on 10 August, although the last Japanese defender did not emerge to surrender until 1960. The Marianas campaign had cost over 22,000 American casualties but the Japanese had lost over 60,000 men.

With the Marianas secured, the chosen Allied targets for the immediate future were the Palaus, which would finally isolate Truk and provide a launching pad for operations into the Philippines and the South China Sea, and the Carolines, which would bring the main fleet bases forward for the Marshalls. Again the operations were to be preceded by widespread carrier strikes but these then revealed that the Philippines were much more lightly held than had been anticipated. As a consequence, the operation against Yap in the Carolines and MacArthur's planned landing on Mindanao were canceled by the Allied planners gathered in Quebec for the Octagon Conference in September 1944 and that against Leyte advanced.

However, it was decided to proceed with the operations against the Palaus which it was erroneously thought were lightly held. On 15 September, therefore, Major General Rupertus' 1st Marine Division of Geiger's III Amphibious Corps met stiff resistance on Peleliu and had to be reinforced by the 81st Infantry Division. The Japanese had now abandoned beach defense and *banzai* attacks in favor of an island-wide in-depth defense and inflicted over 10,400 casualties on the Americans, the last resistance not being overcome by the 81st until as late as November 1944. The other islands in the group, including Angaur, were secured by October while on 23 September elements of the 81st had also landed on undefended Ulithi in the Carolines.

Japan's strategic position was now becoming desperate, with the homeland itself open to direct attack. The first B-29s would strike at Japan from the Marianas on 24 November 1944 – the aircraft that dropped the atomic bomb on Hiroshima would fly from Tinian – and the Americans were free to advance in virtually any direction they chose. And in a significant recognition of the Allies' powerful position, the government of General Tojo that had taken Japan into the war had fallen from office on 18 July 1944.

ABOVE RIGHT: The light cruiser USS *St Louis* bombarding Guam, 21 July 1944.

RIGHT: Gunners of the USS *New Mexico* also participating in the bombardment of Guam.

LEFT: The *New Mexico*'s crew lined up for a meal during a lull in the bombardment.

Allied planning had been sufficiently flexible to enable opportunities to be seized as they occurred and for resources to be switched between MacArthur in the Southwest Pacific and Nimitz in the central region, but it was frequently necessary to conceal the fact from MacArthur lest he hijack the campaign altogether in his personal desire to return to the Philippines. Certainly, MacArthur had been pressing strongly for priority to be given to his advance toward the Philippines rather than to the Central Pacific in the spring of 1944. The seizure of the Admiralties in February 1944 had opened the way for a further advance along the northern coast of New Guinea to Hollandia and thence to Mindanao and Luzon in the Philippines.

The Joint Chiefs of Staff declined to give priority to the Southwest Pacific in March 1944, when they approved the capture of the Marianas, but they did authorize MacArthur to advance to Hollandia. Nimitz was required to provide carrier support for a limited period to allow amphibious landings to be effected both at Hollandia and Aitape where the airfield would be captured to allow air support independent of the carriers. Considerable problems were faced in terms of finding sufficient shipping to support the operation at a time when there were competing demands not only from the Central Pacific but also from Northwest Europe where the Allies were poised to invade Normandy. However, all went ahead on schedule. Units from Lieutenant General Eichelberger's I Corps of General Krueger's Sixth Army landing at Hollandia on 22 April 1944 and elements of Brigadier General Doe's 41st Infantry Division landing simultaneously at Aitape.

While the Japanese had reinforced the Southwest Pacific to some extent in early 1944, they had been unable to spare many troops for the defense of Hollandia and, once more, Allied air power comprehensively destroyed any Japanese aircraft in the area in preliminary raids – some 300 were destroyed at Hollandia in just three days. Accordingly, both Hollandia and Aitape were secured relatively easily, but in July and August 1944 there was a concerted counterattack on Aitape by General Adachi's Eighteenth Army, which was still active in the interior of New Guinea. This necessitated reinforcement of Aitape and tied down forces that MacArthur would liked to have deployed elsewhere. Indeed, the Australians, who replaced the American formations as the latter moved to the Philippines, continued to see action in New Guinea until the end of the war in a campaign that was very bitterly contested.

As it turned out, Hollandia was not as suitable a base for American bombers as had been anticipated and this partly dictated MacArthur's decision to leap ahead to the island of Biak at the mouth of Geelvink Bay by way of Wakde Island off the northern coastal location of Sarmi. Wakde was secured between 18 and 20 May but the landing on Biak on the 27th met fierce resistance which required Eichelberger's personal intervention before the island was declared secure on 20 August. By that time, MacArthur's forces had also seized Noemfoor Island and had landed on the Vogelkop peninsula to complete the clearance of the northern New Guinea coast.

The leap-frogging along the coast had secured a succession of airfields and, for a similar reason, the next advance was to the island of Morotai from which aircraft

PAGES 64-65: The 2nd Battalion, 27th Marines, from the US 5th Marine Division ashore on Iwo Jima, 19 February 1945.

RIGHT: The Japanese carriers *Zuikaku* (center) and *Chitose* during the battle off Cape Engano, 25 October 1944.

BELOW RIGHT: The battleship *Musashi* with other Japanese ships under attack in the Sibuyan Sea, 24 October 1944.

BELOW LEFT: Marine assault craft head toward a beach wreathed in the smoke of the American bombardment at Peleliu in the Palaus, September 1944.

could attack Mindanao. In fact, carrier support would be available for this operation as Nimitz moved in on the Palaus and Carolines in September and Morotai was taken between 15 September and 4 October. It was at this point, however, that the carrier raids on the Philippines revealed Japanese weakness and on 15 September it was decided to cancel MacArthur's planned operations against Mindanao and the Talauds and to go straight for Leyte in October. It was not decided what the next objective would be at that time but MacArthur's plans had been long in preparation and he now envisaged a landing back on Luzon in December.

Once more the Japanese attempted to retrieve the situation by naval action, using carriers as bait and then employing both the battle fleet and land-based aircraft against the American vessels supporting any operations in the Philippine Sea. Yet, from the beginning the Japanese plan was fatally flawed through the prior commitment of many of the trained carrier aircrew available to Formosa and Okinawa, both of which were raided by Halsey's carriers in the run up to the Leyte operation. Over 600 Japanese aircraft were lost either on the ground or in combat with the American fighters. Moreover, the Japanese also lost the battleship *Musashi* and two cruisers on their voyage south through the Sibuyan Sea to aircraft and submarines respectively, although land-based Japanese aircraft also sank the light carrier USS *Princeton*. Nevertheless, in the event, Halsey's Third Fleet carriers were indeed drawn away from immediate support to the Leyte landing force by the Japanese carriers. In the subsequent action off Cape Engano Nimitz's carriers sank the last survivor of the Pearl

Harbor attack, the carrier *Zuikaku*, on 25 October. Halsey's absence exposed Admiral Kinkaid's Seventh Fleet, which was engaged in actions in the Surigao Strait on 24 October and off Samar on the following day.

Together the four actions between 23 and 25 October constituted the Battle of Leyte Gulf, with 282 warships involved it remains the largest naval battle in history. Apart from the *Musashi* and the *Zuikaku*, the Japanese also lost two other battleships, the *Fuso* and the *Yamashiro*, three light carriers, eight more cruisers besides those lost in the Sibuyan Sea and 11 destroyers. As well as the light cruiser already mentioned, the Americans lost two escort carriers and three destroyers. In effect, the Japanese battle fleet had suffered much the same fate as the carrier fleet, and future operations were to be restricted by dwindling fuel supplies. At the same time, with so many trained pilots lost and so little time in which to train replacements adequately, the Japanese now resorted to *kamikaze* ('divine wind') tactics to try and counter American naval superiority. The first such attack took place at Leyte on 25 October, when one of the escort carriers, USS *St Lo*, was sunk.

More losses were inflicted by the suicide attacks when the Americans continued the conquest of the Philippines by landing on Mindoro on 15 December and at Lingayen Gulf on Luzon on 9 January 1945. On 6 January alone 16 Allied ships, including the battleship USS *New Mexico*, were hit. The cruiser HMAS *Australia* was also hit that day for a third time and was eventually struck by no less than six *kamikaze*. In all, 24 vessels were to be sunk and 67 damaged within a month. *Kaiten* suicide boats were also used at Lingayen Gulf.

On land, the fighting was equally hard. On 20 October X and XXIV Corps of Krueger's Sixth Army had landed at Leyte and the Americans were to suffer over 15,000 casualties there between October 1944 and May 1945 despite the fact that Field Marshal Terauchi, commanding Southern Army from Manila, had been denied authority to defend Leyte in depth since Imperial General Headquarters in Tokyo considered that the additional reinforcements they had found for the Philippines should be employed primarily for a decisive battle on Luzon. Initially, therefore, only one division faced the Americans on Leyte, although in early November Tokyo did reverse its decision and the Leyte garrison was reinforced to in excess of three divisions from the Fourteenth Area Army commanded by the effective director of the ground forces in the Philippines and the victor of the campaigns in Malaya and Singapore, Lieutenant General Yamashita. Not only was this too late to save Leyte, which was effectively neutralized by the end of December 1944, but it also threw away divisions which would conceivably have made the subsequent invasion of Luzon that much more difficult.

While Eichelberger, promoted to command a new US Eighth Army in the closing stages of the New Guinea campaign, took over the responsibility for clearing up the last vestiges of resistance on Leyte, Krueger super-

ABOVE: MacArthur returns to the Philippines, 25 October 1944.

ABOVE LEFT: The damage sustained by HMAS *Australia* from a kamikaze aircraft, 21 October.

RIGHT: Shelling has set ablaze a Japanese oil dump as men of the 7th Regiment, US 1st Cavalry Division, advance inland at Leyte, 21 October 1944.

LEFT: A US Coast Guard LST loaded with supplies heads in to the beach at Leyte.

vised the seizure of Mindoro on 15 December to facilitate bringing land-based air power to bear on the subsequent operations on Luzon. Delayed by the resistance encountered on Leyte, the Luzon landing went ahead on 9 January 1945, with US I and XIV Corps establishing a beachhead at Lingayen in the west. The US XI Corps followed farther south on 29 January, with the objective of preventing any Japanese retreat into the Bataan peninsula. Two days later part of the 11th Airborne Division landed at Nasugbu south of Manila. With over 250,000 men available to him, Yamashita conducted a skillful defense which, in fact, eschewed trying to hold either Bataan or the central plains around Manila although, in the event, Rear-Admiral Iwabuchi chose to hold Manila at all costs from his own resources. Instead, Yamashita would hold the mountain areas to the north, west and east of the central plain.

As a result, the initial landing was not significantly opposed and it was some days before the US I Corps on the left of the advance from Lingayen encountered stiffening resistance in the northern mountains. Yamashita's headquarters at Baguio was not taken until the end of April. XIV Corps only ran into major Japanese forces around Bamban in the western mountains on 23 January but these were not brushed aside for another eight days, when Clark Field was secured and the

advance on Manila resumed. However, the American forces then met desperate resistance from Iwabuchi's 17,000-strong naval forces in the capital, and the city was virtually reduced to rubble before it was finally taken on 3 March 1945. Meanwhile, Bataan had fallen quickly and Corregidor was recaptured after a battering from naval and air units, and a coordinated amphibious and airborne assault, on 16 February. The fall of Manila and the clearance of Manila Bay effectively secured Luzon for the Americans but Japanese troops continued to fight in the north until the end of the war, the nature of their resistance being perhaps best illustrated by the fact that Yamashita lost over 205,000 men out of his total garrison while the Americans were to take over 37,000 casualties. Civilians and Filipino guerrillas, who played a major role in the clearing of the Philippines as a whole, also took enormous casualties, a possible 100,000 civilians dying in Manila alone.

MacArthur, who had argued vigorously for the landing on Luzon when Admiral King had favored striking at Formosa after securing Leyte, was now free to turn south toward the Dutch East Indies although it was assumed by the Joint Chiefs that the clearance of the remainder of the Philippines would be achieved primarily by Filipino guerrillas and not American troops. In reality, MacArthur chose to ignore any restrictions on his continuing campaign and, since Eichelberger's Eighth Army was not actually required elsewhere, the Joint Chiefs raised no objections. With most of Luzon secured, Eichelberger therefore went on to clear the rest of the Philippines, beginning with Samar on 19 February and culminating with the landing on Mindanao by US X Corps on 17 April. It was a fragmented campaign against an estimated 100,000 Japanese troops of the Thirty-fifth Army widely scattered through the Philippine archipelago and it necessitated no less than 52 separate amphibious landings between February and 12 July, when a battalion of the US 24th Infantry Division was put ashore at Sarangani Bay to complete the subjugation of Mindanao. Having continued to clear out surviving Japanese garrisons in the Southwest Pacific, Lieutenant General Morshead's Australian I Corps had also been launched into Borneo in May 1945 as the first step toward regaining the Indies.

At the same time that they approved the Luzon invasion in early October 1944 the Joint Chiefs of Staff agreed to a change of direction in the Central Pacific advance toward Iwo Jima in the Bonins and Okinawa in the Ryukyus scheduled for January and March 1945 respectively. Iwo Jima in particular was only 660 miles from Tokyo (approximately three hours by air) and was required as a forward base for bombers operating against Japan, while Okinawa – just 325 miles from Japan – would provide a springboard for an invasion of the Japanese homeland. No one was under any illusion that the Japanese would not fight desperately to hold both islands and, in the case of Iwo Jima, the 3rd, 4th and 5th Marine Divisions of Major General Schmidt's V Amphibious Corps were intensively trained for the task while the island itself was subjected to massive preliminary aerial and naval bombardment.

In fact, the Japanese, who had a reinforced division as well as naval troops on Iwo Jima under the overall command of Lieutenant General Kuribayashi, had been

TOP RIGHT: The USS *Nevada* bombarding Iwo Jima, February 1945.

ABOVE RIGHT: Lieutenant-General Holland Smith and Major-General Schmidt outside V Amphibious Corps headquarters on Iwo Jima, February 1945.

RIGHT: Vice-Admiral Turner (left) with Smith and Schmidt after the securing of Iwo Jima.

ABOVE LEFT: The northern landings on Luzon, January 1945.

working on the defenses for almost eight months when, delayed by the need to give naval support to MacArthur's operations on Luzon, the landing finally went ahead on 19 February 1945. The 4th and 5th Marine Divisions took heavy casualties on the first day and it was to take three days to gain the summit of Mount Suribachi upon which a small patrol raised the American flag on 23 February. This still left the northern half of the island which was honeycombed with caves, bunkers and pill-boxes. It was only on 16 March that the island was declared secure and then another nine days before the last defenders hurled themselves at the Marines in one last desperate and unsuccessful *banzai* attack. The two Marine divisions used in the first landing – the 3rd was landed on 25 February – lost 566 dead and 1755 wounded just coming ashore, and total Marine casualties in an attacking force of some 30,000 men ran at 30 percent in taking an island of only 11.25 square miles. It made Iwo Jima even bloodier than Tarawa and Peleliu for the Americans, while only 1083 out of the Japanese garrison of 23,000 men were taken alive.

The garrison of Okinawa commanded by Lieutenant General Ushijima was over 90,000 strong and, in a massively complex operation involving no less than 1457 ships, 183,000 men of Lieutenant General Buckner's Tenth Army were allocated for the subjugation of the island. After the occupation of some outlying islands the II Amphibious Corps and XXIV Corps landed on the west coast on 1 April 1945. The landings went well because

Ushijima had chosen to wage a prolonged defensive battle in the interior and, as on Luzon, it was some days before the Americans came up against the main Japanese defenses around Shuri in the south, where limestone hills honeycombed with caves presented a formidable barrier to the attacker. It was only penetrated once the Americans began to use flamethrowers and explosives to blast the Japanese from their hiding places. A major Japanese counterattack around Kishaba failed on 12/13 April and another around the Kochi ridge on 4/5 May. The bitterly contested struggle continued as the Japanese steadily withdrew from one defensive position to another until abandoning the main Shuri line between 22 and 30 May. Even then the fighting did not end until 22 June.

Once more the Japanese had also massed *kamikaze* and *kaiten* to oppose the supporting American fleet, and the battleship *Yamato* was also despatched on a suicide mission with just enough fuel to reach Okinawa. Since the loss of her sister ship, *Musashi*, at Leyte, the *Yamato* was the largest and most powerful battleship afloat but she never got to fire her 18-inch main armament in anger for repeated American aircraft attacks sank her in the Van Diemen Strait on 7 April with the loss of all but 269 of her 3322-strong crew in what was to prove the Japanese Navy's last action. Nonetheless, *kamikaze* took out 21 Allied ships and crippled 43 others between 6 April and 22 June, while the operation as a whole proved one of the costliest of the Pacific War for the Americans

RIGHT: An American flamethrower blasts Japanese defenses blocking the way to Iwo Jima's Mount Suribachi.

BELOW: Men of the 28th Marines, 5th Marine Division, raise the flag on Mount Suribachi.

BELOW RIGHT: Japanese dead on Iwo Jima, 20 February 1945.

BELOW LEFT: Under heavy fire, Marines inch forward up the slope of Red Beach on Iwo Jima, 19 February 1945.

with over 12,000 dead and 36,000 wounded among both soldiers and seamen. However, the Japanese lost another 110,000 dead and over 4000 aircraft, including almost 2000 shot down during *kamikaze* missions. It also cost the lives of both Buckner, who had been killed by Japanese artillery fire while visiting a forward observation post on 18 June, and Ushijima, who committed suicide with his chief of staff four days later.

The pressure on Japan was also increasing in other ways. Allied submarines had been wreaking havoc on the Japanese merchant fleet. By August 1945 it had been reduced to barely 1.5 million tons compared to its peak of 5.5 million tons in mid-1942. In the last year of the war, too, a concentrated attack was begun on the Japanese oil tankers on which her economy depended, while the fishing fleet was unable to put to sea with a consequent

heavy blow being dealt to a large part of a population whose staple diet was fish. Lack of imports equally affected agriculture and industry while output generally was also hit by the American bombing of Japan, which had commenced from Chinese airfields in June 1944 and, as already related, from the Marianas in November 1944. The first targets of the new B-29 Superfortresses flying from the Chinese mainland were Japanese aircraft factories but in February 1945 the Americans switched to fire raids on major population centers. On the night of 9 March such a raid on Tokyo resulted in 83,793 deaths and the same treatment was meted out to other cities in succeeding months, the bombers receiving additional protection from April onward from fighters based on Iwo Jima. At least 241,000 Japanese

TOP LEFT: The USS *Idaho* fires its broadside against Okinawa, March 1945.

TOP RIGHT: Nimitz and Spruance (wearing the sun helmet) coming ashore on Okinawa.

ABOVE LEFT: A Curtiss SC-1 float-plane taxis up to a landing mat to be picked up by the USS *Alaska*'s crane off Iwo Jima, 6 March 1945.

ABOVE: Japanese surrendering on Okinawa.

were killed in Allied raids and it is estimated that over 8.2 million had to be evacuated from the cities.

The strategic bombing of Japan undoubtedly strengthened a more moderate faction with the leadership in Tokyo which now wanted peace, but there was still every likelihood of appalling Allied casualties – perhaps as high as a million – if the Allies were compelled to invade Japan to end the war. That invasion – Operation Downfall – was a matter of some controversy within Allied planning circles, the US Army favoring a direct invasion and the US Navy preferring a slower blockade. In June 1945 something of a compromise emerged with an intensified blockade and bombardment to be followed by an invasion scheduled to begin with a landing on Kyushu ('Olympic') by US Sixth Army in November 1945 and on Honshu ('Coronet') by the US 8th and 1st Armies – the latter comprising the US XXIV and III Amphibious Corps – in March 1946. In the event, of course, other developments were to intervene.

The creation of the atomic bombs dropped on Hiroshima and Nagasaki was the culmination of a long series of key scientific developments stretching back beyond Hahn's breakthrough in discovering the fission process in 1938 to Rutherford's splitting of the atom in 1919. By 1939 scientists in Britain, France and the United States were moving toward investigating the military potential of nuclear energy. In Britain in particular work progressed to an extent which excited American interest when it was revealed to them in mid-1941. In October of that year it was agreed to pool resources given the possibility that Germany might be attempting to produce a bomb first. It became clear that only the United States had the necessary capabilities to make a bomb and the Manhattan Project was formally established in June 1942 under the direction of Lieutenant General Groves. It enabled the simultaneous pursuit of five different pos-

sible alternative routes to producing a device at a variety of sites including Oakridge in Tennessee, Hanford in Washington State, the University of Chicago and, later, Los Alamos in New Mexico. After the expenditure of some $2000 million a bomb was successfully tested near Alamogordo in New Mexico on 16 July 1945, the so-called Interim Committee having recommended its use on 1 June.

Having given the Japanese an opportunity to respond to surrender terms agreed among the Allies at the Potsdam Conference, President Truman – Roosevelt had died on 12 April – authorized use of the bomb on 28 July. At 0811 hours on 6 August the B-29 'Enola Gay' dropped the first bomb, the 9000lb 'Little Boy' with a destructive power of 20,000 tons of high explosive, on Hiroshima.

ABOVE RIGHT: Paul Tibbetts with his B-29 *Enola Gay*.

RIGHT: The devastation after the dropping of the atomic bomb on Nagasaki.

Generating a force of blast of 8.0 tons per square yard and an estimated heat at ground zero of 6000°C the bomb killed between 70,000 and 80,000 people and injured between 80,000 and 130,000 to a varying extent. With the Japanese still unable to agree on surrender, a second bomb, nicknamed 'Fat Man' and with similar characteristics to the first, was dropped on Nagasaki three days later. It killed between 20,000 and 35,000 and injured between 50,000 and 60,000 people. More had died in the fire raids on Tokyo and other cities but, of course, these raids did not have the implications of the release of radiation over Hiroshima and Nagasaki.

While the dropping of the atomic bombs convinced Emperor Hirohito that peace was now necessary, the military still resisted surrender. On the day before Nagasaki was bombed, however, the Soviet Union had finally adhered to a pledge given at the Allied conference at Yalta in February 1945 and declared war on Japan. In return the Soviet leader, Stalin, had extracted the price of being awarded those territories lost by Imperial Russia after its defeat by the Japanese in the Russo-Japanese War of 1904-5 and the Kurile Islands Russia had ceded to Japan in 1875. He had also secured at least a tacit Allied acquiescence in his policies in Eastern Europe. Truman did not have his predecessor's somewhat naive view of Stalin's trustworthiness and would have preferred the war to have ended before Soviet troops could enter Manchuria. Consequently, the decision to drop the bomb certainly embraced an element of due warning to the Soviet Union occurring as it did during the Potsdam Conference. Indeed, a number of Truman's advisers believed that the Japanese would surrender without American recourse to the bomb.

The Soviet entry to the war was in itself an additional pressure on the Japanese since, drawing on the lessons of the last four years, the Red Army advanced into Manchuria in a model Soviet-style blitzkrieg. The once much-vaunted Kwantung Army that had initiated the Mukden Incident 14 years previously was smashed within days, although Soviet operations continued until 20 August 1945. The Japanese Army still refused to concede defeat even after the Soviet entry and elements even attempted a coup d'etat just before the emperor and his government were to announce their decision to surrender on 15 August 1945. When Hirohito broadcast the decision to his people at noon that day, it was the first time that most Japanese had ever heard his voice.

ABOVE: The atomic cloud rises over Nagasaki, 9 August 1945.

LEFT: MacArthur is just visible at right of the table with his back to the camera as the Japanese sign the surrender terms on the USS *Missouri*, 2 September 1945.

CONCLUSION

The official surrender ceremony to end the Pacific War took place on the battleship USS *Missouri* in Tokyo Bay on 2 September 1945. Among those present as MacArthur, the designated Commander of the Allied Powers, took the surrender were Wainwright and Percival who had been forced to capitulate almost four years previously at Corregidor and Singapore respectively. But even this was not the final act for there were the consequences of victory and defeat to be faced by both Allies and Japanese alike.

At the time of the emperor's broadcast. Japan still had 2.3 million men under arms in the Japanese homeland islands, excluding the various reserves, quasi-military formations and militia that amounted nominally to a further 28 million. In addition, there were some 3.5 million Japanese troops and 3.1 million Japanese civilians in the Pacific and Asian theaters. Similarly, there were an estimated 1.2 million slave laborers – mostly Korean – in Japan, while the Allies also had to deal with the recovery of prisoners of war and internees. To give one example of the practical problems involved, when the boundary of Admiral Lord Louis Mountbatten's South East Asia Command was extended in August 1945 to embrace those parts of the Dutch East Indies formerly in MacArthur's South West Pacific Area – it already included Burma, Thailand, Malaya, Singapore and Sumatra – it meant that Mountbatten would have to plan for the disarming and demobilization of some 738,000 Japanese troops over an area of 1.5 million square miles and the simultaneous recovery of over 71,000 Allied PoW's or internees. It was also a time when shipping was in relatively short supply and the Allies themselves were faced with demands for rapid demobilization from wartime servicemen.

In such circumstances, it often meant that Japanese troops continued to be armed under Allied command so as to maintain law and order until such time that sufficient numbers of Allied troops could be found and despatched to take control themselves. At the time that Mountbatten left South East Asia Command in May 1946, for example, there were still more than 64,000 Japanese troops under arms in his area and in both French Indochina and Java the Japanese had been required to fight alongside Allied – primarily British – forces against nationalists. Indeed, the shortage of Allied troops had encouraged nationalists such as the MPAJA in Malaya and the Viet Minh in French Indochina to emerge and disarm the Japanese themselves. In French Indochina Ho Chi Minh proclaimed an independent Democratic Republic of Vietnam in Hanoi on 2 September 1945. Indonesian nationalists on Java had similarly declared their independence from the Dutch on 17 August. In the case of French Indochina, the first British troops did not arrive in Saigon until 11 September, or on Java until 29 September.

Ultimately, of course, the French and Dutch possessions were to win their independence in bitter struggles against the returning colonial powers, while the British had already acknowledged the need to concede independence to India, Burma and Ceylon as the United States had similarly already promised independence to the Philippines. In fact, the Americans had to assist the newly independent Filipino government to beat off an insurgent challenge from the Huks just as the British authorities in Malaya were to face an insurgent challenge from the communist elements that had formerly comprised the MPAJA. Elsewhere, the arrangement in the Korean peninsula whereby the Soviets disarmed the

RIGHT: Two emaciated Allied prisoners of war collect their meager belongings after being freed from the camp at Aoimori near Yokohama, 28 August 1945.

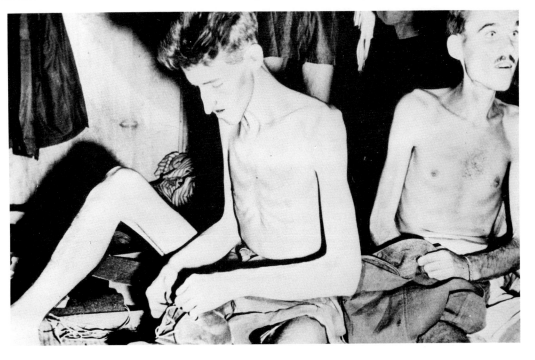

Japanese north of the 38th Parallel and the Americans, who only arrived there on 8 September, south of the parallel was to result in a *de facto* partition. This was despite the intention expressed by Allied foreign ministers in December 1945 that steps be taken to unify Korea under a trusteeship, independence having been agreed at both the Cairo Conference in November 1943 and at the Potsdam Conference.

While the Soviets also occupied Sakhalin, Port Arthur and the Kuriles, the former Japanese mandates in the Pacific were assumed by the United States: Iwo Jima was returned to Japan in 1968 and Okinawa in 1972. In China, of course, the removal of the Japanese brought about the intensification of the civil war between the nationalist government of Chiang Kai-shek and the communists of Mao Tse-tung, culminating in Mao's triumph in 1949.

Japan itself passed under an occupation by 250,000 Allied (mainly American) troops (Operation Blacklist) under the direction of MacArthur, who was to enjoy virtual proconsular powers in Tokyo until his dismissal during the Korean War. Unconditional surrender had been demanded by the Allies on 26 July 1945 during the Potsdam Conference without any reference being made to the future status of the emperor. Subsequently, however, in reply to a Japanese overture on 10 August, which indicated her willingness to capitulate, the Allies implied that Hirohito would be permitted to remain as emperor. The price, however, was the divesting of the power of the emperor and the establishment of what amounted to a constitutional monarchy. At the same time the Japanese constitution was extensively redrawn and society transformed by such measures as the enfranchisement of women, the granting of civil liberties, land reform, the breaking up of financial monopolies, the encouragement of trade unions and the abolition of that form of the Shinto religion that encouraged worship of the emperor and his predecessors. Militarism was effectively outlawed with the new constitution which came into effect in May 1947 renouncing the use of force in international relations.

There was also a series of war crime trials held by an International Military Tribunal for the Far East sitting in Tokyo between April 1946 and April 1948 and other regional tribunals. In all, some 4400 individuals were tried by the various tribunals resulting in 954 death sentences. Most defendants were categorized as lesser Class C war criminals but 20 field commanders including Yamashita, who was hanged, were categorized as Class B offenders with 25 – another two had died and one was declared insane – in the Class A category tried by the main Tokyo tribunal. Most of these were cabinet ministers or soldiers who had served in the government Seven were condemned to death, including six soldiers of whom the most prominent was Tojo and one politician. They were hanged in December 1948.

The reform of Japan facilitated agricultural and industrial progress and enabled the country to achieve an economic miracle in the 1950s following the peace treaty concluded with the Allies in 1951 but the Pacific War itself brought considerable economic disruption throughout the Far East. It was also immensely costly in terms of lives, the war against Japan embracing not only the Pacific campaigns recounted in this volume but the British campaign in Burma brought to a successful con-

TOP: The victor and the vanquished. MacArthur meets Hirohito after the Japanese surrender.

ABOVE: Still allies – Colonel Barrett, a US observer, pictured with General Chu-teh (left) and Mao Tse-tung.

clusion by Slim's Fourteenth Army, which had retaken Rangoon in May 1945, and the almost equally forgotten war that had raged in China ever since 1931. In World War II as a whole (and including action in China since 1937), some 1.7 million Japanese servicemen were killed together with approximately 400,000 Japanese civilians, but such losses were dwarfed by the upward of 10 million dead in China. British and Imperial losses in Southeast Asia totaled 227,313 land casualties while American casualties in the Pacific theater amounted to 291,543, of whom 100,997 were killed.

The total loss of life throughout the Pacific and Southeast Asian theaters is all but impossible to calculate. What is clear, however, is the enduring global significance of what transpired in the Pacific between December 1941 and August 1945, not least in the way it ended at Hiroshima and Nagasaki.

Page numbers in *italics refer to illustrations.*

Admiralty Islands 26, 44, 66
Akagi, carrier 14, 26, 31
Aleutian Islands 26, 28, 30, 52, *52, 53*
Alexander, General Harold 22
Anti-Comintern Pact (1936) 9
USS *Arizona*, battleship 17
atomic bomb development of 75 Hiroshima 62, 75-76 Nagasaki 75, *75,* 76, *76*
Australia 20, 21, 26, 27, 36, 44
HMAS *Australia*, cruiser 67, *69*
Australian Army 19, 42, 43, *43,* 44, 66, 71

B-17 bombers 17, 20, 21, 31
B-25 bombers 27, *27*
B-29 bombers 58, 62, 74 'Enola Gay' 75, *75*
Barrett, Colonel *78*
Bataan 20, 21, *21,* 70
Blamey, Sir Thomas 42, 43
Bose, Subhas Chandra 23
Bougainville *34-35,* 43, *46, 47, 48,* 49, *49*
Boxer Rebellion (1900) 7
Britain 7, 8, 10, 11, 14, 52, 75
British Army 18, 19, 22, 78
Buckner, Lieutenant General Simon 72, 73
Burma 14, 22, 23, *23,* 52, 53, 77, 78

USS *California*, battleship 17
Canadian Army 19
Caroline Islands 8, 26, 52, 53, 58, 59, 62, 67
Casablanca Conference (1943) 52
Ceylon 26, 77
Chiang Kai-shek 78
China 7, 8, 9, 10, 11, 14, 26, 27, 49, 53, 74, 78
Chinese Army 22
Chinese Communist Army *78*
Chu-Teh, General *78*
Coral Sea, Battle of the (1942) *24-25,* 28, *28, 29,* 30, 41
Corregidor 21-22, *21, 22,* 70, 77
USS *Cowpens*, carrier *50-51, 55*
Curtiss SC-1 float-plane *74*

Doolittle, Lieutenant Colonel James *26,* 27
Douglas SBD-111 Dauntless dive-bombers *30,* 31, *33*
Douglas TBD-1 Devastator torpedo-bombers 31
Dutch East Indies 10, 11, 14, 19, 22, 23, 26, 70, 77

Eichelberger, Lieutenant General Robert 42, 66, 68, 71
'Enola Gay,' B-29 bomber 75, *75*
USS *Enterprise*, carrier 30, 32, 37, 39

F6F Hellcat fighter plane *55, 59*
Filipino troops 21, *21,* 70

Fletcher, Rear Admiral Frank 28, 30, 31, 37
Formosa 7, 14, 52, 58, 67, 70
Forrestal, James *57*
France 7, 8, 9, 75 *see also* Indochina

Germany 7, 8, 9, 36, 52
Gilbert Islands 14, 22, 26, *50-51,* 52, 53, *55,* 56, 60
Guadalcanal 36, *36,* 37, *37, 38,* 39-41, *39, 41,* 42, 43, 44, 53
Guadalcanal, naval Battle of (1942) 40, *40*
Guam 14, 19, *60,* 62, *63*

Halsey, Vice-Admiral William F 30, 43, 44, 49, 52, 67
Hirohito, Emperor of Japan *11,* 76, 77, 78, *78*
Hiroshima, dropping of atomic bomb on (1945) 62, 75-76, *78*
Hiryu, carrier 14, 26, 32, *32*
Ho Chi Minh 23, 77
Homma, General Masaharu 14, 20, *20*
Hong Kong 14, 19, 52
USS *Hornet*, carrier *26,* 27, *27,* 30, 32, *33,* 37, 39, *39*
Hutton, Lieutenant General Thomas 22
Hyakutate, Lieutenant General Harukichi 41, *41*

USS *Idaho*, battleship *74*
India 19, 22, 26, 77
Indian Army 18, 19, 22, 23
Indochina 9-10, 14, 23, 77
Iwo Jima *4-5, 64-65,* 71-72, *71, 72, 73,* 74, *74,* 78

Java 19, 21, 22, 53, 77

Kaga, carrier 14, 31
kaiten missions 67, 72
kamikaze missions 67, *68,* 72, 73
Kimmel, Admiral Husband 14, 17, 27
King, Admiral Ernest 36, 52, 70
Konoye, Prince Fumimaro *11*
Korea 7, 40, 77-78
Krueger, General Walter 43, 66, 68

League of Nations 8, 9
USS *Lexington*, carrier 28, *29*
Leyte 67, 68, *68, 69,* 70, 72
Leyte Gulf, Battle of (1944) 67, *67*
Luzon 20, 58, 66, 67, 68, 70, *71,* 72

MacArthur, Lieutenant General Douglas 20, 21, *21,* 36, 41, 42, 43, 52, 58, 59, 62, 66, 67, *69,* 70, 72, *76,* 77, 78, *78*
Malaya 14, 18-19, *18,* 22, 23, 53, 68, 77
Manchuria 7, 8, 14, 53, 76
Manhattan Project 75
Manila 20, 21, 70
Mao Tse-tung 78, *78*
Marianas Islands 8, 52, 53,

58-59, *59,* 62, 66, 74
Marshall Islands 8, 27, 52, 53, 54, 56, *56, 57,* 58, *58,* 60, 62
USS *Maryland*, battleship *12-13,* 17
Maw, Dr U Ba 23
Meiji Restoration (1868-1912) 7
Midway, Battle of (1942) 27, 28, 30-32, *30-33,* 41
Mikuma, cruiser 32, *33*
USS *Missouri*, battleship Japanese surrender on *76,* 77
Mitscher, Admiral Marc *26*
USS *Monterey*, carrier *54, 59*
Mountbatten, Admiral Lord Louis 77
Mukden Incident (1931) 9, 76
Musashi, battleship 67, *67,* 72

Nagasaki, dropping of atomic bomb on (1945) 75, *75,* 76, *76,* 78
Nagumo, Vice-Admiral Chuichi 14, *14,* 26, 30, 31, 62
USS *Nevada*, battleship 17, 71
New Georgia 43, 44, *44*
New Guinea 22, 26, 27, 36, 40, 41-42, *42,* 43, *43,* 52, 53, 59, 66
USS *New Mexico*, battleship *62, 63,* 67
Nimitz, Admiral Chester 27, 28, 30, 36, 37, 42, 54, 56, 59, 66, 67, 74
Non-Aggression Pact (1941) 9

Octagon Conference, Quebec (1944) 62
Okinawa 67, 71, 72, *74,* 78

P-38 Lightning fighters 49
Palau Islands 58, 59, 62, 67
Pearl Harbor, attack on (1941) *1,* 11, *12-13,* 14, *14, 15, 16,* 17, *17,* 67
USS *Pennsylvania*, battleship *1,* 17
Percival, General Arthur 19, 77
Perry, Commodore Matthew *6,* 7
Philippine Sea, Battle of (1944) 59, *59*
Philippines 10, 14, 17, 20-22, *20, 21, 22,* 23, 49, 52, 58, 62, 66, 67-68, *68, 69,* 70, 71, *71,* 72
Phillips, Admiral Sir Tom 18
Port Moresby 26, 27, 28, 41-42
Potsdam Conference (1945) 75, 76, 78
USS *President Jackson*, transport *40*
HMS *Prince of Wales*, capital ship 18, *19*
prisoners-of-war 21, 40-41, 77, *77*

Quadrant Conference, Quebec, (1943) 52

Rabaul 26, 27, 28, 36, 37, *41,* 43, 44, *48,* 49, 52, 53, 58

Roosevelt, President Franklin D 10, 21, 75
Rupertus, Major General William 62
Russia 7, 8, *see also* Soviet Union
Russo-Japanese War (1904-05) 7, *7,* 14, 76
Ryujo, light carrier 26, 37

USS *St Louis*, light cruiser *63*
Saipan 59, 60, *60, 61,* 62
San, Aung 23
Santa Cruz engagement (1942) 39, *39*
USS *Saratoga*, carrier 20, 30, 37, 39
Schmidt, Major General Harry 57, 71, *71*
Sextant Conferences, Cairo and Tehran (1943) 54, 58, 78
Shoho, carrier 27, 28, *28*
Shokaku, carrier 14, 26, 27, 28, *29,* 37, 39, 59
Short, Lieutenant General Walter 14, 17
Singapore 14, 18, 19, *19,* 22, 23, 68, 77
Sino-Japanese Wars (1894) *6,* 7 (1937) 9, *9*
Slim, Lieutenant General William 22, 78
Smith, Major Holland 'Howling Mad' 53, 60, *71*
Smith, Major General Julian 53
Smith, Major General Ralph 53, 60
Solomon Islands *2-3,* 22, 26, 27, 36, 40, 43, 44, *44,* 49, 52, *see also* Bougainville, Guadalcanal
Soryu, carrier 14, 26, 31
Soviet Union 9, 14, 26, 53, 76, *see also* Russia
Spruance, Rear Admiral Raymond 30, 31, 53, 54, *57,* 59, *74*
Stalin, Josef 76
surrender by Japan 75, 76, 78, *78* in Pacific *76,* 77

Tarawa 53-54, *54, 56,* 72
USS *Tennessee*, battleship *12-13,* 17
Thailand 14, 18, 22, 77
Tibbetts, Paul 75
Tojo, General Hideki 11, *11,* 62, 78
Tokyo 7, 11, 17, 23, 68, 75, 74, 76, 78,
Doolittle raid (1942) 74, 76
Trident Conference Washington, (1943) 52
Tripartite Pact (1940) 9
Truk 26, 49, 52, 56, 58, 59, 62
Truman, President Harry 75, 76
Tulagi 26, 27, 28, 37, 39
Turner, Vice-Admiral Richmond *71*
Ushijima, Lieutenant General Mitsuru 72, 73
USS *Utah*, battleship 17

Vandegrift, Major General *36*,
37, 39
Viet Minh 23, 77

Wainwright, Lieutenant
General Jonathan 22, 77
Wake Island 14, 20, *20*, 27, 59
war crime trials 78
Washington Conference (1921-
22) 8
USS *Wasp*, carrier 37, 39, *39*
Wavell, General Sir Archibald
19, 22
USS *West Virginia*, battleship
12-13, *15*, *16*, 17
Wildcat fighters 31, 37

World War I 8, *8*

Yalta Conference (1945) 76
Yamamoto, Admiral Isoroku 14,
26, 28, 30, 32
Yamashita, General Tomoyuki
14, 68, 70, 78
Yamato, battleship 30, 72
Yangtze Incident (1937) 10, *10*
USS *Yorktown*, carrier 28, *29*,
30, *30*, *31*, 32, *33*

Zero fighters 31
Zuikaku, carrier 14, 16, 27, 28,
37, 59, *59*, 67, *67*

ACKNOWLEDGMENTS
The author and publishers
would like to thank Ron Callow
for designing this book and Pat
Coward for compiling the
index. The following agencies
and individuals provided
photographic material:
Australian War Memorial,
page: 69(top).
Bison Books, pages:
16(bottom), 21(top left),
71(bottom), 75(top), 76(top),
78(top).
Robert Hunt Library, pages:
2, 6(bottom), 7(bottom),
8(both), 9(both), 10-11(top),
11(bottom), 18(both), 19(all
three), 20(bottom), 21(top
right & bottom), 22(left), 27,
42, 43(top), 52, 68(top), 70,
77, 78(bottom).
**Imperial War Museum,
London,** pages: 17, 23,
43(bottom).
**Peter Newark's Historical
Pictures,** page: 6(top).
US Air Force Photographs,
pages: 32(bottom),
61(bottom).
US Army Photographs,
pages: 34, 57(bottom),
69(bottom).
US Coastguard Photographs,
page: 68(bottom).
**US Defense Photographs
(Marine Corps),** pages:
41(both), 45, 48(top), 49,
54(top), 56(bottom), 57(top),
60(both), 61(top), 64, 66, 72,
73(all three), 74(bottom
right), 76(bottom).
US National Archives, pages:
1, 22(right), 29(both), 30,
32(top), 33(both), 36(bottom),
37, 38(both), 39(both),
40(both), 46(both), 47(both),
53, 54(bottom), 55(both),
56(top), 58(both), 59(both),
67(top), 74(both left).
US Naval Photographs,
pages: 10(bottom), 12, 14,
15(both), 16(top), 20(top), 24,
26, 28, 31, 44, 48(bottom),
50, 62, 63(both), 67(bottom),
71(top & middle), 74(top
right), 75(bottom).